Against All Odds

Recent titles in Teacher Ideas Press
Readers Theatre Series

Judge for Yourself: Famous American Trials for Readers Theatre
Suzanne I. Barchers

Just Deal with It! Funny Readers Theatre for Life's Not-So-Funny Moments
Diana R. Jenkins

How and Why Stories for Readers Theatre
Judy Wolfman

Born Storytellers: Readers Theatre Celebrates the Lives and Literature of Classic Authors
Ann N. Black

Around the World Through Holidays: Cross Curricular Readers Theatre
Written and Illustrated by Carol Peterson

Wings of Fancy: Using Readers Theatre to Study Fantasy Genre
Joan Garner

Nonfiction Readers Theatre for Beginning Readers
Anthony D. Fredericks

Mother Goose Readers Theatre for Beginning Readers
Anthony D. Fredericks

MORE Frantic Frogs and Other Frankly Fractured Folktales for Readers Theatre
Anthony D. Fredericks

Songs and Rhymes Readers Theatre for Beginning Readers
Anthony D. Fredericks

Readers Theatre for Middle School Boys: Investigating the Strange and Mysterious
Ann N. Black

African Legends, Myths, and Folktales for Readers Theatre
Anthony D. Fredericks

Against All Odds

Readers Theatre for Grades 3-8

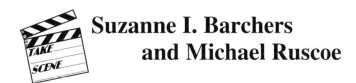

Suzanne I. Barchers
and Michael Ruscoe

Readers Theatre

Teacher Ideas Press

An imprint of Libraries Unlimited
Westport, Connecticut • London

Library of Congress Cataloging-in-Publication Data

Barchers, Suzanne I.
    Against all odds : readers theatre for grades 3-8 / Suzanne I. Barchers and Michael Ruscoe.
      p. cm. — (Readers theatre)
    This book presents 25 readers theatre scripts.
    Includes bibliographical references.
    ISBN 978-1-59158-677-7 (alk. paper)
    1. Celebrities—Conduct of life—Juvenile drama. 2. Perseverance (Ethics)—Juvenile drama. 3. Conduct of life—Juvenile drama. 4. Children's plays, American. 5. Readers' theater. 6. Drama in education. 7. Perseverance (Ethics)—Study and teaching (Elementary)—Activity programs. 8. Character—Study and teaching (Elementary)—Activity programs. 9. Conduct of life—Study and teaching (Elementary)— Activity programs. I. Ruscoe, Michael. II. Title.
    PS3552.A5988A68   2008
    812'.54—dc22   2007048817

British Library Cataloguing in Publication Data is available.

Library of Congress Catalog Card Number: 2007048817
ISBN: 978-1-59158-677-7

First published in 2008

Libraries Unlimited/Teacher Ideas Press, 88 Post Road West, Westport, CT 06881
A Member of the Greenwood Publishing Group, Inc.
www.teacherideaspress.com
www.lu.com

Printed in the United States of America

The paper used in this book complies with the
Permanent Paper Standard issued by the National
Information Standards Organization (Z39.48–1984).

10 9 8 7 6 5 4 3 2 1

To Josh and Jen Barchers, who love a challenge.
—SIB

With love to Benji, the best reader I know.
—MR

Contents

Introduction

Tom Cruise, Lance Armstrong, Halle Berry—these are all are names of famous people the public has grown to admire. Although students may know that Tom Cruise is a famous film star, they may not realize that he struggles with reading. Lance Armstrong fought cancer. Halle Berry faced prejudice during her career. These are just three examples of the thirty-one people profiled in twenty-five scripts, all people who have faced and overcome incredible challenges. They are ideal for inspiring students who face academic, physical, or emotional challenges.

Scripts found in *Against All Odds: Readers Theatre for Grades 3–8* have been developed from biographies, autobiographies, news articles, and Internet sources. Although the essential facts of each person's story have been carefully researched, the conversations are largely fictional. The authors searched for a variety of people worthy of inclusion. The scripts are short, covering only a few aspects of the person's life. Two of the scripts, "They All Beat the Odds" and "Special Guests," briefly profile four people each, providing students with opportunities for further research.

Each script has been evaluated using the Flesch-Kincaid readability formula for grade level. Once the proper names have been eliminated, the scripts have a readability level of Grades 2 or 3. The scripts are ideal for remedial or developing readers.

Using Readers Theatre

Readers theatre can be compared to radio plays. The emphasis is on an effective reading of the script rather than on a dramatic, memorized presentation. Students may paraphrase the scripts, and this should be encouraged. In some scripts, the narrators have long passages, and they should rehearse their lines carefully. Reading orally develops strong reading skills, and listening to scripts promotes active listening for students in the audience. The scripts also provide an opportunity for preparing a special program or for a diversion from the regular curriculum.

Preparing the Scripts

Once scripts are chosen for reading, make enough copies for each character, plus an extra set or two for your use and a replacement copy. To help readers keep their place, have students use highlighter markers to designate their character's role within the copy. For example, someone reading the role of Narrator 1 could highlight the lines in blue, with another character highlighting the lines in yellow.

Photocopied scripts will last longer if you use a three-hole punch (or copy them on pre-punched paper) and place them in inexpensive folders. The folders can be color-coordinated to the internal highlighting for each character's part. The title of the play can be printed on the outside of the folder, and scripts can be easily stored for the next reading. The preparation of the scripts is a good project for a student aide or volunteer parent. The preparation takes a minimum of initial attention and needs to be repeated only when a folder is lost.

Getting Started

For the first experience with a readers theatre script, choose a script with many characters to involve more students. Gather the students informally. Ask the students what they know about the person who is the subject of the script. Share any articles you might have about the person. Next, introduce the script and explain that readers theatre does not mean memorizing a play and acting it out, but rather reading a script aloud with perhaps a few props and actions. Select volunteers to do the initial reading, allowing them an opportunity to review their parts before reading aloud. Discuss how the scripts are alike or different from what you and the students know about the person. Write pronunciations on the board of any challenging names or words. While these students are preparing to read their script, another group could be reviewing another script or brainstorming ideas for props or staging.

Before reading the first script, decide whether to choose parts after the reading or to introduce additional scripts to involve more students. A readers theatre workshop could be held periodically, with each student belonging to a group that prepares a script for presentation. A readers theatre festival could be planned for a special day when several short scripts are presented consecutively, with brief intermissions between each reading. Consider grouping together related scripts. For example, scripts about athletes, such as David Eckstein, Oksana Baiul, and Kurt Angle, could be presented together.

Once the students have read the scripts and become familiar with the new vocabulary, determine which students will read the various parts. Some parts are considerably more demanding than others, and students should be encouraged to volunteer for roles that will be comfortable for them. Once they are familiar with readers theatre, students should be encouraged to stretch and try a reading that is challenging.

Presentation Suggestions

For readers theatre, readers traditionally stand—or sit on stools, chairs, or the floor—in a formal presentation style. The narrators may stand with the script placed on music stands or lecterns slightly off to one or both sides. The readers may hold their scripts in black or colored folders. The position of the reader indicates the importance of the role. On occasion, key characters might sit on high stools to elevate them above numerous other characters. The scripts include a few suggestions for presentation, but students should be encouraged to create interesting arrangements.

Props

Readers theatre has no, or few, props. However, simple costuming effects will lend interest to the presentation. Students should be encouraged to decide how much or little to add to their reading. For some readers, the use of props or actions may be distracting, and the emphasis should remain on the reading rather than on an overly complicated presentation.

Delivery Suggestions

Delivery suggestions generally are not imbedded in the scripts. Therefore, it is important to discuss with the students what will make the scripts come alive as they read. During their first experiences with presenting a script, students are tempted to keep their heads buried in the script, making sure they don't miss a line. Students should learn the material well enough to look up from the script during the presentation. Students can learn to use onstage focus—to look at each other during the presentation. This is most logical for characters who are interacting with each other. The use of offstage focus—the presenters look directly into the eyes of the audience—is more logical for the narrator or characters who are uninvolved with onstage characters. Alternatively, have students who do not interact with each other focus on a prearranged offstage location, such as the classroom clock, during delivery. Simple actions can also be incorporated into readers theatre.

Generally the audience should be able to see the readers' facial expressions during the reading. On occasion, it might seem logical for a character to move across the stage, facing the other characters while reading. In this event, the characters should be turned enough so that the audience can see the reader's face.

The Next Step

Students who are particularly inspired by the stories they have read in this book should be encouraged to do further reading about the plays' subjects. Each play includes suggested sources. Some are for adult reading; preview to determine appropriateness. Students can also be assigned writing projects based on these plays. For example, students can write letters to the people who have inspired them most. In these letters, students can relate their own experiences of overcoming obstacles and how a certain celebrity's story moved or inspired them. Once students have enjoyed the reading process involved in preparing and presenting readers theatre, they can create their own scripts. Encourage students to research other people for scripts.

Useful Web sites for researching people with learning disabilities or other challenges include the following:

- http://sachem.suffolk.lib.ny.us/advisor/bioadversity.htm (A list of biographies and autobiographies about people who beat the odds)

- http://www.eas.wayne.edu/fam_people.html (A list of famous people with disabilities)

Kurt Angle

Wrestler

Summary

Kurt Angle grew up in a blue-collar, roughneck town near Pittsburgh, Pennsylvania. After Kurt's father died in a construction accident, his brothers became involved in drugs and alcohol. His sister became pregnant at age sixteen.

This play tells the story of how Angle overcame the odds to become not only an Olympic gold medal winner but also perhaps the greatest amateur wrestler the sport has ever seen. Later, Kurt moved on to the world of sports entertainment. He became one of the most popular stars in professional wrestling. Although he often plays the bad guy in the ring, Angle uses his spare time to encourage young people to make the most of their lives.

Presentation Suggestions

To get the feel for the environment in which Angle excelled, this play could be read in the school gym, where amateur wrestling mats could be set up. Before or after reading the play, a physical education teacher could explain (and perhaps show) the differences between amateur wrestling and the professional wrestling with which students might be more familiar.

Related Books and Media

- Angle, Kurt, and Jon Harper. *It's True! It's True!* New York: Regan Books/ HarperCollins, 2001.

- Schaefer, A. R. *Olympic Hero: Pro Wrestler Kurt Angle*. Greenwood, IN: Capstone Press, 2002.

- The National Wrestling Hall of Fame and Museum: www.wrestlinghalloffame.org

Characters

Narrator 1

Narrator 2

Eric Angle, *Kurt's brother*

Kurt Angle

Mrs. Angle, *Kurt's mother*

Mark Angle, *Kurt's brother*

Doctor 1

Steve, *a college friend of Kurt's*

Doctor 2

Wrestling Judge

Abbas Jaddi, *a world-class Iranian wrestler*

Announcer 1

Announcer 2

Fan 1

Fan 2

Student 1

Student 2

Kurt Angle
Wrestler

Scene 1

Narrator 1: It is late August 1984. Kurt Angle is sixteen. He is walking home with his older brother, Eric.

Eric Angle: Something wrong, Kurt?

Kurt Angle: Yeah. I stink, that's what's wrong. The first year I wrestled, I was 2 and 14. I haven't gotten much better since then. I want to be as good as you, Dave, Mark, and John.

Eric Angle: Just because your older brothers are good wrestlers doesn't mean you have to be one, too. Remember, Kurt—you're as tough as they come. And you'll prove it to yourself one day.

Narrator 2: The boys arrive home. Their mother is waiting for them. She's very upset.

Mrs. Angle: Boys, we have to hurry. There's been an accident at the construction site. Your father's on the way to the hospital. Let's go!

Narrator 1: Soon, Kurt, Eric, and their mother arrive at the hospital.

Mrs. Angle: Is there any news?

Mark Angle: Not yet. But the guys from the site told me that Dad fell fifteen feet from his crane.

Kurt Angle: Well, Dad's tough. He's always careful. It can't be that bad, can it?

Mark Angle: The guys … they said that he landed on his head.

Kurt Angle: I don't care. This is Dad. He'll pull through somehow.

Narrator 2: The family waits for hours. Finally, a doctor arrives in the waiting room.

Doctor 1: I wish I had better news for you all. Your father has suffered a severe injury. He's in a coma. He's not going to come out of it.

Mrs. Angle: Oh, no …

Doctor 1: I'm afraid that he is brain-dead. You'll have to decide how long you want the machines to keep him alive.

Narrator 1: Mrs. Angle breaks into tears. Soon the rest of the family does as well.

Narrator 2: The next day, the family decides to take Mr. Angle off of the life-support machines. Before they do, each family member takes a moment to say goodbye in private. Soon, it's Kurt's turn. He stands by his father's bed.

Kurt Angle: Dad … I don't know what to say. I guess … I just want to say thanks. Thanks for being there for me. Thanks for being at all my games and matches, even after working twelve-hour days. Thanks for driving me so hard. Sometimes … I got really mad about that. But I know you only wanted me to do my best.

Narrator 1: When Kurt speaks again, he speaks firmly.

Kurt Angle: I promise I'll always do the best I can, Dad. I'll always make you proud. I swear it.

Scene 2

Narrator 2: It is 1988. Kurt is a freshman at Clarion College in Pennsylvania.

Narrator 1: On a Friday night, Kurt is in his dorm room. He is reading a book on wrestling technique. Steve, a friend of his, sticks his head in the room.

Steve: Kurt! You're going to the party later, aren't you?

Kurt Angle: What party?

Steve: There's a party at Sam's apartment! There will be girls and beer. It'll be a blast.

Kurt Angle: No, thanks.

Steve: You're going to pass up the biggest party of the year to stay here and read a book?

Kurt Angle: No. I'm going to sleep soon. I have to be back at the gym early tomorrow.

Steve: You drive yourself too hard, man. Come out and have some fun.

Kurt Angle: I am having fun. I love wrestling, especially now that I'm pretty good at it.

Steve: Yeah, but I'm talking about *real* fun, Kurt.

Kurt Angle: You know, my brothers and sisters go to parties all the time. Now, my brothers are hooked on drugs and booze. And my sister is pregnant at sixteen. My brothers were some of the best athletes I ever saw. They threw it all away. I'm not going to make that mistake.

Steve: Fine. But when we're out of college, I'm going to have a lot of great memories to look back on. What will you have?

Kurt Angle: *(smiling)* Gold. I'm going to have gold.

Scene 3

Narrator 2: Kurt goes on to win the NCAA wrestling championships in his sophomore and senior years. After college, Kurt piles up medals in amateur wrestling contests around the world. He looks to compete in the 1996 Olympic Games. They are to be held in Atlanta, Georgia.

Narrator 1: In 1995, he competes in Atlanta for amateur wrestling's world championship and a spot on the U.S. Olympic team. During his match, his opponent flips him in the air, and Kurt lands on his neck.

Narrator 2: Kurt calls for a time-out. He talks to his brother, Mark, who is coaching him. Kurt is in agony.

Mark Angle: What's the matter with you?

Kurt Angle: My neck … I did something to it. It's really bad!

Mark Angle: Hey, suck it up, Kurt. You're behind in points. Now get back out there and score!

Narrator 1: Somehow, Kurt drops his opponent to the mat at the buzzer. The move gives him a point. He wins the decision, 4 to 3.

Narrator 2: Later, Kurt and Mark see a doctor about Kurt's neck.

Doctor 2: I've looked at the x-rays. I'm amazed you were able to get through that match, Kurt. You've cracked two bones in your neck. You're done with wrestling, son. For good.

Kurt Angle: No … that's impossible …

Doctor 2: I'm sorry.

Narrator 1: The doctor leaves the room.

Mark Angle: Don't worry. I'll go talk to him. There must be something we can do.

Narrator 2: Mark leaves. Kurt stares at the floor. Finally, he breaks into tears.

Scene 4

Narrator 1: Kurt and Mark see several doctors. One doctor says that he can give Kurt injections to numb his neck pain. But he also tells Kurt that he could be seriously hurt if his neck is injured again.

Narrator 2: Kurt goes for his Olympic dream. At the 1996 games, he reaches the finals against Abbas Jaddi. Jaddi is a great Iranian wrestler. He outweighs Kurt by twenty-nine pounds. Still, the two wrestle to a 1-to-1 tie. The winner of the match must be chosen by a vote of the three-referee panel.

Narrator 1: Angle stands in the middle of the ring. He is exhausted. Jaddi stands by the referee's table.

Wrestling Judge: Jaddi, get back in the ring!

Narrator 2: Jaddi catches a glimpse of one of the referees' cards. The ref has voted for Jaddi.

Abbas Jaddi: Yes! I am the winner!

Kurt Angle: *(to himself)* No way! I out-wrestled him! *I know it!*

Narrator 1: The judge pulls Jaddi back into the ring. He takes a wrestler's wrist in each hand. In a moment, he will lift the winner's arm in victory.

Announcer: The winner of the gold medal in freestyle wrestling in the 240-pound class … by a two-to-one vote of the referees—

Narrator 2: Jaddi begins to lift his own arm in victory.

Announcer 1: From the United States of America, Kurt Angle!

Abbas Jaddi: *What?*

Narrator 1: The crowd goes wild. Kurt's family celebrates in the stands. Angle drops to his knees. He raises his arms in victory as tears stream down his face. The crowd chants Kurt's name, along with "U-S-A! U-S-A!"

Kurt Angle: This is for you, Dad! This is for you!

Scene 5

Narrator 2: Five years have gone by. Thousands of pro wrestling fans pack an arena in Pittsburgh, Pennsylvania. It is Kurt's hometown.

Announcer 2: Ladies and gentlemen, please welcome the World Wrestling Entertainment Champion, Kurt Angle!

Narrator 1: Kurt makes his way to the ring in an explosion of music and fireworks. A gold medal hangs around his neck. He wears the WWE title belt around his waist. The crowd erupts in boos and catcalls.

Fan 1: You stink, Angle!

Fan 2: You don't deserve the belt!

Narrator 2: Kurt smiles and holds his hands up in victory. In the ring, he picks up a microphone.

Kurt Angle: My friends, your Olympic hero and your WWE champion accepts your warm welcome home!

Narrator 1: The crowd boos again. Kurt is playing the "heel," or the bad guy, in the wrestling show.

Kurt Angle: I know you're all glad to see me, because let's face it: I'm the only good thing in sports that Pittsburgh has going. I mean, the Pirates. The Steelers. The Penguins. They're all awful!

Narrator 2: The boos grow louder. Many members of the crowd, though, are laughing as well.

Kurt Angle: Let's be honest. Your lives are *pathetic*! And if it weren't for me, you'd have *nothing* to live for! Oh, it's true— it's true!

Narrator 1: Angle smiles. He holds his arms up in triumph once again. Boos and jeers rain over him.

Narrator 2: Suddenly, the scene freezes on a television screen. Kurt is in a Pittsburgh classroom. He is showing the scene from the wrestling show to a group of students.

Kurt Angle: Pretty mean stuff, huh?

Narrator 1: The students laugh.

Kurt Angle: Sometimes, I play the "baby face," or good guy. Most of the time, though, my character is the bad guy, the "heel."

Student 1: Does anyone ever confuse the character of Kurt Angle with who you are in real life?

Kurt Angle: Oh, sure. I'll be walking down a street, and someone will get in my face and scream, "You stink, Angle!"

Student 2: Don't you get mad?

Kurt Angle: Not at all. I just say, "Hi, I'm Kurt. I'm not really the jerk you saw on TV last night. I'm a real human being."

Narrator 2: The students laugh.

Kurt Angle: My job is to do my best to entertain our fans. A long time ago, I promised my father that I would do my best at whatever I did. And doing your best doesn't have anything to do with belts or medals or titles. It has to do with being a champion in life.

Narrator 1: Kurt looks over the students.

Kurt Angle: Whatever you're doing in school, at home, and for the rest of your lives, you should *always* do your best. Believe me—it's worth it.

Cross Outs

Kurt Angle

	A	B	C
1	x-ray	injection	victory
2	wrestlers	pin	celebrate
3	loss	hopes	on
4	boos	catcalls	winning

1. Cross out the word for a picture of bones in row 1.

2. Cross out the word for what you do when you win in column C.

3. Cross out 2 words in row 4 for what people do when they jeer or show their dislike.

4. Cross out the word for a "win" in column C.

5. Cross out the word for the opposite of a win in column A.

6. Cross out the word for a shot given with medicine in column B.

Write the remaining words in order below.

_____ _____ _____ _____

_____.

Lance Armstrong

Cyclist

Summary

Lance Armstrong and his mother, Linda, supported each other through difficult years. Linda essentially raised him alone. Lance was an active, often difficult child. However, Linda believed in him and loved him fiercely. Lance continued to be devoted to his mother for her unwavering support as he built his biking career. When Lance was diagnosed with testicular cancer, he thought his bicycle racing career was over. More devastating was learning that the cancer had spread to his brain. Brain surgery and chemotherapy followed, with debilitating results. Still, Lance battled back to win the Tour de France for the seventh year in a row in 2005. Note: the specifics of the type of cancer have been omitted. If students are mature enough, discuss the nature of testicular cancer and how Armstrong's treatment included the removal of a testicle.

Presentation Suggestions

Use a biking theme for the stage. Lance and Linda should be in the center of the stage with the other characters on either side.

Related Book and Media

- Armstrong, Lance, and Sally Jenkins. *It's Not About the Bike: My Journey Back to Life*. New York: Berkley, 2001.

- www.lancearmstrong.com

Characters

Narrator 1

Narrator 2

Narrator 3

Lance Armstrong

Linda Armstrong, *Lance's mother*

Doctor

Chris, *Lance's coach*

Rick, *Lance's friend and doctor*

Dr. Reeves

Lance Armstrong Cyclist

Scene 1

Narrator 1: Lance lives with his mother when he is a little boy. She raises him alone. They don't have much money, but they are happy. Then his mom gets married. Lance doesn't like his stepfather, Terry Armstrong. They live in Plano, Texas. Lance is twelve years old.

Lance Armstrong: Mom, I want to join the swim club.

Linda Armstrong: Son, go ahead and try if you want to.

Narrator 2: Lance goes to the first meeting of the swim club. He's probably the worse swimmer in the group.

Narrator 3: Lance tries hard. He practices a lot. The coach helps him and pushes him to do better. One year later, Lance competes in the 1,500-meter freestyle at the state meet. He wins fourth place.

Linda Armstrong: Lance, I'm so proud of you! Your work paid off.

Lance Armstrong: Thanks, Mom. I just read about something I'd like to try next.

Linda Armstrong: What's that?

Lance Armstrong: It's a race that combines biking, swimming, and running. It's called a triathlon. I've been biking to practice everyday. I should be able to do well.

Linda Armstrong: We'll need to get you a better bike then.

Narrator 1: Linda takes Lance to get a racing bike. Lance wins the race. Then he races in another triathlon and wins that too. He may not be the best swimmer or a good football player, but he finds out he's the best in the state at triathlons.

Scene 2

Narrator 2: Lance continues to race a lot. As he gets older, he does things that make his stepfather angry. Sometimes he rides his bike just to get away from home.

Narrator 3: One day his mother tells him that she is getting a divorce.

Linda Armstrong: Lance, Terry is leaving. We're getting a divorce.

Lance Armstrong: That's great, Mom.

Linda Armstrong: Son, I don't want you to give me any problems.

Lance Armstrong: I won't, Mom. That guy is no good.

Narrator 1: Lance tries to help out his mom. They don't have much money. She doesn't have a great job. But she doesn't give up. Lance keeps winning triathlons—and money.

Lance Armstrong: Mom, I want you to have the prize money from the race.

Linda Armstrong: Lance, that's your money.

Lance Armstrong: No, Mom, it's our money. Take it.

Narrator 2: Lance starts entering bike races. There are four classes of races. He starts in category four, the lowest. Soon he's racing in category one races.

Linda Armstrong: Lance, you're doing well at the racing. You have a future with this. But you have to give it 110 percent.

Lance Armstrong: I will, Mom.

Linda Armstrong: You'll need to be really organized. Make check lists. Be sure you have everything you need for every race.

Lance Armstrong: I think I can get sponsors soon. That will help with the money.

Linda Armstrong: I'm sure you can, Lance. Just remember, you have to do the races yourself. I'll help you all I can with other things.

Narrator 3: Linda does help Lance. They travel together to the races. He begins making pretty good money.

Scene 3

Narrator 1: Lance loves to train. But he also takes risks. He weaves in and out of traffic. Sometimes he runs stoplights. One time he races across six lanes of traffic. The light changes, and a driver hits him. Lance is taken to the hospital.

Doctor: Son, you have a concussion. We had to stitch up your head too. You need to rest.

Lance Armstrong: I have a triathlon in six days.

Doctor: You also have a gash in your foot. No racing for you. You can't do anything for three weeks. Stay off your feet.

Lance Armstrong: Okay, doctor.

Narrator 2: Lance goes home and rests. He gets bored in two days. He decides to sign up for the triathlon.

Narrator 3: Lance borrows a bike. He removes the stitches out of his foot himself. He cuts holes in his shoes so he can run and bike.

Narrator 1: He takes third in the triathlon.

Scene 4

Narrator 2: Lance graduates from high school. He gets to be on the U.S. national team and compete at races around the world. His coach, Chris, gives him advice at his first big race in Japan.

Chris: I want you to hang back. Don't get up front in the wind. You'll get tired too fast.

Lance Armstrong: Okay, coach.

Narrator 3: Lance doesn't listen to Chris. He wants to prove how good he is. He races to the front of the pack.

Chris: *(to himself)* What is he doing?

Narrator 1: Lance finds out that Chris was right. He gets tired halfway through the race. He finishes in 11th place.

Chris: Congratulations, Lance. That was the best finish ever by an American.

Lance Armstrong: Thanks, Coach.

Chris: But you could have done better. If you had held back you would have won a medal. You can be a world champion. But you have a lot of work to do.

Lance Armstrong: What do I have to do?

Chris: You have to be stronger than everyone else. And you have to learn *how* to race.

Narrator 2: Lance trains hard. He learns what he needs to know about racing. He wins an important race in Italy for the U.S. national team.

Chris: Lance, you've learned how to race well. One day you're going to win the Tour de France.

Narrator 3: When Lance is twenty-one years old, he competes in the World Championships. He wins the race. He and Linda celebrate his hard work. Then Lance goes right back to training.

Scene 5

Narrator 1: By 1996, Lance is twenty-five years old. He has fought hard to win many important races. But his biggest battle is about to start. And it isn't a bike race.

Narrator 2: Lance begins to feel sick. He has a sore throat. It hurts when he sits on the bike seat. He has trouble breathing. But he keeps going. He is talking on the phone to his friend Bill one day and starts coughing up blood. He calls his doctor, who lives nearby.

Lance Armstrong: Rick, could you come over? I'm coughing up blood.

Narrator 3: Rick comes over and checks Lance's nose and mouth.

Rick: It could be bleeding from your sinuses.

Lance Armstrong: That's probably what it is.

Narrator 1: Lance is relieved. At first he doesn't tell Rick that he's had other symptoms. But a couple of days later, he feels worse. He is so uncomfortable on his bike seat that he can hardly ride. He tells Rick.

Rick: You need to get checked out. I'll call a doctor for you.

Narrator 2: Lance goes to see Dr. Reeves. The doctor orders x-rays and other tests. Lance waits uneasily. Finally, he calls Rick about his symptoms.

Lance Armstrong: Rick, I don't know what's going on. They won't tell me. I have to see Dr. Reeves again.

Rick: I'll come down. I'll meet you at his office.

Narrator 3: By the time the tests are done, it is late. Dr. Reeves shows Lance and Rick the x-rays.

Dr. Reeves: This is serious. You have cancer, and it has spread to your lungs.

Lance Armstrong: Are you sure?

Dr. Reeves: I'm sure. You should have surgery as soon as possible.

Narrator 1: Dr. Reeves explains the surgery and treatment. He leaves Lance and Rick alone to talk.

Rick: Lance, cancer can be cured. You can beat this.

Lance Armstrong: Okay. Let's do this. Whatever it takes …

Narrator 2: Lance then makes one of the hardest calls he has ever made. He calls his mom to tell her he has cancer.

Scene 6

Narrator 3: Lance has surgery. Later he begins chemotherapy. He and Linda read everything they can about cancer. He tries to eat the right foods. He exercises even when he feels bad. He even keeps riding his bike.

Narrator 1: Then Lance is told he needs to have another test. The doctors want to test for brain cancer. They find two spots on his brain. Only eight days have passed since Lance learned he had cancer.

Narrator 2: Lance and Linda are in shock. But they begin to study their choices. In another week, Lance has brain surgery. Chris comes to see him after the surgery.

Chris: How are you doing?

Lance Armstrong: I'm great.

Chris: Yeah, right …

Lance Armstrong: Really, Chris. This is just one more thing I'm going to beat. I know I can do it.

Narrator 3: The surgery is a success. His race sponsors continue to support him. Lance is feeling positive about his future. Then he starts chemo again. He feels sick most of the time. Sometimes he can hardly walk. He gets discouraged. But he gets through all the chemo.

Narrator 1: Then he has to wait to see if the chemo worked. He won't know for a year. For months he thinks he'll never race again. He gradually returns to biking, and life gets better and better.

Narrator 2: In 1998, Lance gets married and takes fourth place in the World Championship road race.

Narrator 3: In 1999, Lance's son is born—and he wins the Tour de France. He wins the Tour again in 2000. In 2001, he not only wins once more but also becomes the father to twin girls.

Narrator 1: In 2002, Lance wins the Tour de France for the fourth time. He has proven to the world that he can beat cancer—and still win races. And in 2003, Lance races in the Tour de France for the fifth time. He is knocked off his bike when he hits a woman's purse at a corner. A fellow biker in the race stops until Lance can get back on to race again. He wins for the fifth time.

Narrator 2: Lance breaks all records. He wins in 2004 and 2005—seven times in a row! That is his last win. He decideds to quit racing in the Tour de France after "lucky seven."

Cross Outs

Lance Armstrong

	A	B	C
1	France	beating	United States
2	cancer	chemo	takes
3	triathlon	hard	Tour de France
4	lung	work	brain

1. Cross out the word for cancer treatment in column B.

2. Cross out the names of 2 countries in row 1.

3. Cross out the 2 words in row 4 for the surgeries Lance had.

4. Cross out the names of 2 races in row 3.

Write the remaining words in order below.

_____ _____ _____ _____

_____.

Oksana Baiul

Figure Skater

Summary

No other figure skater has lived such a rags-to-riches story as Oksana Baiul. Baiul was born in Ukraine in the former Soviet Union in November 1977. Her parents split up when she was two. At age thirteen, Oksana lost her mother to cancer. With no one to turn to, Oksana was taken in by skating coach Galina Zmievskaya. She was the mother-in-law of Victor Petrenko. Petrenko, a great Ukranian skater, had already won two Olympic medals.

In the span of two years, Oksana became a world-class figure skater. She won the world title in 1993. At the 1994 Olympics, sports fans were focused on a scandal involving American skaters Nancy Kerrigan and Tonya Harding. Oksana seemed to come out of nowhere to win the gold medal.

Oksana, however, had trouble adjusting to her newfound celebrity and the wealth that came with it. After the Olympics, she turned professional. Then she moved to Simsbury, Connecticut, along with a group of Ukraine skaters. But Oksana spent too much time exploring the freedom that her wealth and fortune gave her. She had an alcohol-related auto accident in 1997. In 1998, she joined an alcohol rehabilitation program. Today, Oksana is once again reclaiming her life. While she still skates for fun and fitness, she now works on her own line of skating clothing. Once again, she is on the road to success.

Presentation Suggestions

While reading this play, teachers and students could watch tapes of Oksana's performances on the ice. Students can also research various skating terms (jump, flip, toe-loop, axel, etc.) before reading the play.

Related Books and Media

- Baiul, Oksana, and Heather Alexander. *Oksana: My Own Story*. New York: Random House, 1997.

- Baiul, Oksan, Simon Bruty, and Christopher Sweet. *Secrets of Skating: Oksana Baiul*. New York: Universe Books, September 1997.

- The United States Figure Skating Association Online: www.usfsa.org

Characters

Narrator 1	Medic
Narrator 2	Police Officer 1
Galina Zmievskaya, *a Ukranian skating coach*	Police Officer 2
Victor Petrenko, *a Ukranian figure skater*	Reporter
Oksana Baiul	

Oksana Baiul
Figure Skater

Scene 1

Narrator 1: The year is 1992. At a practice rink in Ukraine, world-champion Victor Petrenko skates off the ice. He meets with his coach and mother-in-law, Galina Zmievskaya.

Galina Zmievskaya: Not bad, Victor. You were awkward landing your triple toe-loop, though.

Victor Petrenko: I know. I hit a bad patch of ice. Our team has had so much success. You'd think the government would fix up the rink.

Galina Zmievskaya: Times are tough, Victor. Master the bad ice. It will make you better on the good ice in other countries.

Victor Petrenko: Very well. Let me get out of my skates and into my shoes. I'll give you a ride home.

Narrator 2: Victor goes to a locker area. At the other end of the room, he sees someone lying on a cot under a pile of old blankets. Victor walks over to the cot.

Victor Petrenko: Excuse me?

Narrator 1: The person in the cot turns over. It is thirteen-year old Oksana Baiul.

Victor Petrenko: I've seen you skate here before. You are Oksana, yes?

Oksana Baiul: That's right.

Victor Petrenko: I've never seen anyone take a nap at the rink. Are you all right?

Oksana Baiul: I'm . . . fine. It's just that . . . my mother has died. I live here now.

Victor Petrenko: Oh, Oksana. I'm so sorry. Isn't there anyplace you can go?

Oksana Baiul: My father left us years ago. My grandparents are dead. I have no other family.

Victor Petrenko: Come. Come with me.

Narrator 2: Victor brings Oksana outside. There, he explains her problems to his mother-in-law.

Galina Zmievskaya: You poor child. This is no way for a girl to grow up.

Oksana Baiul: I don't know what else to do.

Galina Zmievskaya: Victor said that you skate. Are you good?

Oksana Baiul: I suppose . . .

Galina Zmievskaya: Then I would be happy to coach you, if you like.

Oksana Baiul: *(thrilled)* You? I would be honored!

Galina Zmievskaya: Good. But I don't coach homeless girls. Come home with me. We'll get you cleaned up and fed. You can meet my daughters.

Scene 2

Narrator 1: Oksana moves into Galina's home. Soon, she becomes a great skater. In her first competition, the Nation's Cup Games, she places fourth. In 1993, she wins a silver medal in the European Championship.

Narrator 2: She wins a gold medal at the World Championship in 1993. Soon, she is training for the 1994 Olympic Winter Games.

Narrator 1: There, the focus of the world is on two American skaters, Nancy Kerrigan and Tonya Harding. Kerrigan was a favorite for the Olympic gold medal. A couple of months earlier, though, an unknown attacker had struck her in the knee with a steel bar. Rumors that Harding was behind the attack swirled through the news.

Narrator 2: At a practice session, all eyes are on Kerrigan and Harding—except for the eyes of Oksana's coach, Galina. She mumbles to herself as she watches Oksana.

Galina Zmievskaya: Good, Oksana. Good. Be patient. Set up for your jump. Excellent!

Narrator 1: Galina sees Oksana heading for another skater. Oksana doesn't see the other skater in her path.

Galina Zmievskaya: Oksana! Look out!

Narrator 2: The two skaters crash into each other. They are helped off the ice. Oksana is in tears.

Medic: What is it, Oksana? Tell us what hurts.

Oksana Baiul: I cut my leg with my skate. And my back, and shoulder—I twisted them.

Medic: Try to relax. Let us take care of you.

Narrator 1: The cut in Oksana's leg is stitched. She's given painkillers for her other injuries.

Narrator 2: Then it's time to skate her final program. As she waits to take the ice, her friend Victor talks to her.

Oksana Baiul: I don't know if I can do this.

Victor Petrenko: You can do it, Oksana. Many times I have skated through pain. Now you must. You are stronger than your pain. And this is your moment.

Narrator 1: Oksana smiles at him. Her name is called. She takes the ice. Kerrigan has already skated. She leads the competition. Oksana's program begins with a slight mistake. Within moments, though, she is skating much better.

Narrator 2: Oksana knows she needs something extra to beat Kerrigan. She adds a triple toe-loop to her program. She also adds a difficult double-axel, double toe-loop combination. The moves come late in her program, when most skaters would be too tired to do them.

Narrator 1: She leaves the ice and joins her coach. They wait for the judges' results. Oksana is in tears again.

Galina Zmievskaya: What is it, child? You skated beautifully!

Oksana Baiul: *(sobbing)* My mother. She is with me. I could feel my mother on the ice with me.

Narrator 2: Moments later, the judges' decision is announced. It is the closest women's figure skating result in history. Oksana wins the gold. Galina throws her arms around her.

Galina Zmievskaya: You won! The gold medal is yours!

Narrator 1: Oksana falls into Galina's arms as the two weep in victory.

Narrator 2: Soon after, Oksana turns pro. Along with Victor, Galina, and a group of other Ukraine figure skaters, she moves to Simsbury, Connecticut. The group trains at a new skating center.

Narrator 1: Oksana works a frantic schedule. She trains. She skates with a traveling ice show. She makes commercials. She earns millions of dollars. She goes on a wild shopping spree. She buys herself clothes, jewelry, a $500,000 home, and a new sports car.

Narrator 2: She also begins to drift away from Galina and Victor. She begins hanging around with new friends. For the sixteen-year-old girl with no family, sudden fame and fortune become a tough burden to bear.

Scene 3

Narrator 1: It is a cold night in January 1997. Two police officers respond to an accident on a dark road near Hartford, Connecticut.

Police Officer 1: There it is. A green Mercedes. Looks like it just ran off the road.

Police Officer 2: What a wreck! It must have been doing over 100.

Officer 1: Call an ambulance—I'll check on the driver.

Narrator 2: The officer opens the car's front door. Oksana is behind the wheel. Blood flows from a cut on her forehead.

Officer 1: Are you all right, ma'am?

Oksana Baiul: *(woozy)* Where . . . where am I?

Officer 1: You've been in an accident, ma'am. Try not to move. Help is on the way.

Oksana Baiul: *(seeing her blood)* I'm bleeding . . . I'm going to die!

Officer 1: No, you're not. Don't worry. Just try to relax.

Narrator 1: The other officer looks through the paperwork in the glove compartment.

Officer 2: I smell alcohol. We'll need to—hey! You know who this is? Oksana Baiul.

Officer 1: The skater? Really? *(to Oksana)* Miss? Miss Baiul? Stay with us, OK?

Oksana Baiul: No. No, I don't want to be me anymore. I'm so tired . . . so tired of it all . . .

Narrator 2: Oksana is charged in the accident. She agrees to go through an alcohol education program. The charges are dropped.

Narrator 1: Oksana still struggles with her life, She finds skating difficult. She begins drinking again. In May 1998, she enters an alcohol rehabilitation facility. She vows to turn her life around for good.

Scene 4

Narrator 2: It is March 2003. Oksana is now twenty-five. She sits down with a newspaper reporter in New York City.

Oksana Baiul: There was one night, five years ago. I was tossing and turning in bed, crying. I was supposed to skate the next day, but I couldn't go on. I was too scared. Too weak. I knew that if I didn't change my life, I would die.

Reporter: And how are you doing today?

Oksana Baiul: Today, my life is wonderful. I'm engaged to a great man. And I've started my own line of fashion clothing for figure skating.

Reporter: Do you still skate?

Oksana Baiul: I skate now for fun and to keep myself in shape. I will always love skating. I'm still proud of winning the gold medal. But I had no idea how it would affect my life.

Reporter: How do you look back at those years now—the years after you won the gold?

Oksana Baiul: I learned a lot about who I am, and who I wanted to be. Sometimes I act like a much older person. And sometimes I still feel like a little kid. A kid who's been through a lot.

Cross Outs

Oksana Baiul

	A	B	C
1	some	skaters	double toe-loop
2	Olympics	live	silver
3	World Championship	on	ice
4	judges	edge	gold

1. Cross out the two colors of medals in column C.

2. Cross out the name of a skating move in row 1.

3. Cross out the name of people who choose the winners in row 4.

4. Cross out what skaters skate on in row 3.

5. Cross out the names of two competitions in column A.

Write the remaining words in order below.

_____ _____ _____ _____

_____.

Halle Berry

Actress

Summary

In 1991, actress Halle Berry was given her first screen role. She played a crack addict in the movie *Jungle Fever*. Just over ten years later, Berry stood at the top of the Hollywood ladder. She gained an Academy Award nomination for her role in the film *Monster's Ball*.

The story of Berry's rise to success is as dramatic as the roles she plays in the movies. She is the daughter of a black father and a white mother. She has fought against racism all her life—from her hometown near Cleveland, Ohio, all the way to Hollywood. She also struggled in her relationships with men. Her father was abusive. She suffered through a nasty public divorce.

Her resolve, though, saw her through troubled times. It also helped make her one of the biggest stars in show business. Today, life is truly sweet for Halle Berry.

Presentation Suggestions

During the play, the room could be decorated with posters and pictures from some of Berry's films (*Jungle Fever*, *The Program*, *The Flintstones*, *Introducing Dorothy Dandridge*, *X-Men*, *Die Another Day*). Students can also research and put up pictures of the African American stars Berry most admired while growing up (Dorothy Dandridge, Lena Horne, Diahann Carroll).

Related Books and Media

- Farley, Christopher. *Introducing Halle Berry*. New York: Pocket Books, 2002.

- Naden, Corrine J., and Rose Blue. *Halle Berry: Black Americans of Achievement*. New York: Chelsea House, 2002.

- Hallewood: The Official Web Site of Halle Berry: www.hallewood.com

Characters

Narrator 1

Narrator 2

Halle Berry, *an actress*

Judith Berry, *Halle's mother*

Russell Crowe, *an actor*

Nick

Brenda

Dan

Vicki

Casting Director

Vincent Tirrincione, *Halle's manager*

Studio Boss

Halle Berry
Actress

Scene 1

Narrator 1: The 2002 Academy Awards Ceremony is being held in Hollywood, California. The Academy Awards (nicknamed the "Oscars") are being handed out for excellence in motion pictures. All of the movies' biggest stars are there. Millions around the world watch on TV.

Narrator 2: Actress Halle Berry sits with her mother at the ceremony. They have sat through a long show. Finally, the Oscar for Best Actress is about to be announced.

Halle Berry: I still can't believe this is happening!

Judith Berry: I'm so nervous!

Narrator 1: Actor Russell Crowe takes the stage.

Russell Crowe: Ladies and gentlemen, I have the honor of announcing the winner for Best Actress. The nominees are: Halle Berry, in *Monster's Ball* . . .

Narrator 2: The crowd applauds wildly. Halle is their clear favorite.

Russell Crowe: Judi Dench, in *Iris* . . .

Narrator 1: The audience applauds once more.

Russell Crowe: Nicole Kidman, in *Moulin Rouge* . . .

Narrator 2: Again, the crowd applauds.

Russell Crowe: Sissy Spacek, in *In the Bedroom* . . .

Narrator 1: More applause washes over the room.

Russell Crowe: And Renee Zellweger, in *Bridget Jones's Diary*.

Narrator 2: There is more applause. Then the auditorium falls silent. Crowe opens the envelope that contains the name of the winner.

Russell Crowe: And the Oscar goes to . . .

Judith Berry: My goodness, Halle. Think. Think about everything it took to get you here . . .

Narrator 1: Suddenly, everything seems to go in slow motion. Halle's mind drifts back to the early years of her life.

Scene 2

Narrator 2: Halle sees herself as a child. She is sitting alone at a table in a school cafeteria. Most of the other kids are white. Halle's mother is white, and her father is black. Her father was physically abusive. He left Halle, her sister, and her mother when Halle was only four.

Narrator 1: Two boys, Nick and Dan, and two girls, Brenda and Vicki, stand to one side of the lunchroom. They whisper and laugh. Finally, they all step over to Halle and sit down at the table.

Nick: Hi, Halle. Mind if we join you?

Halle Berry: I guess not . . .

Brenda: Great! What do you have for lunch today, Vicki?

Vicki: Oh, hamburger, fries. What about you, Dan?

Dan: Yeah, same thing. Topped off by a nice, cold glass of milk.

Nick: Hey, Dan—are you *sure* that's milk?

Dan: Yeah. Why?

Brenda: Didn't you put *chocolate* in your milk?

Dan: I guess so.

Vicki: Well, once you take white milk and you put some chocolate in it, it's not *really* milk anymore, is it?

Narrator 2: The four children look at Halle and wait for her reaction. She glares at them. They all burst out laughing.

Narrator 1: Halle angrily gets up and leaves.

Narrator 2: Later that night, Halle is still upset. She talks to her mother about what happened.

Halle Berry: I was so angry! I just wanted to fight them all!

Judith Berry: You can't do that, sweetheart. You're my daughter, which means you're half white. But when you leave this house, people will think you're black. So accept being black. Embrace it. If you fight it, you'll not only have a battle with them. You'll have a battle inside yourself, too.

Narrator 1: Halle feels the wisdom in her mother's words. She smiles.

Halle Berry: Thanks, Mom.

Scene 3

Narrator 2: Several years later, Halle has graduated from high school. She tries for a career in acting and modeling. She goes to many auditions but has trouble landing roles. She also marries a young baseball player. His career takes off. Halle, however, struggles to find work.

Narrator 1: One day, she visits a casting director. He is looking for an actress to fill a part.

Casting Director: Can I help you?

Halle Berry: Yes. I'm Halle Berry. My manager sent me to read for a part.

Casting Director: Oh. *You're* Halle Berry? I was expecting . . . a different actress.

Halle Berry: Well, can I read for the part anyway?

Casting Director: I don't know . . .

Halle Berry: Is there any reason I *shouldn't* read for the part?

Casting Director: No, of course not. It's just . . . we weren't thinking about going black for this part.

Halle Berry: Excuse me? "Going black?"

Casting Director: It's nothing personal. Really.

Halle Berry: Just give me a chance. I think I can do it.

Casting Director: Listen, honey, we're wasting our time here. The part is for a park ranger. I don't even think there are any black park rangers, are there?

Halle Berry: *What?* You don't think that there are any . . . okay. Fine. Thanks anyway.

Narrator 2: She slams the door as she leaves. Soon, she's in the office of Vincent Tirrincione, her manager.

Halle Berry: He said he didn't think there were any black park rangers! What is going on in these people's brains?

Tirrincione: Look, we just have to keep on trying. I want you to go read for a Spike Lee in New York City. He's a young director, and his films are very powerful.

Narrator 1: Halle wins the part in Lee's film. She plays a crack addict who loses her child because of her drug problem. Additional film roles come slowly but surely. Meanwhile, Halle is having problems off the screen.

Narrator 2: One night, Halle calls her mother from California.

Halle Berry: Mom, I don't know how to tell you this, but . . . David and I are getting a divorce.

Judith Berry: Oh, I'm sorry, Halle. Did he . . . did he hit you?

Halle Berry: It wasn't as bad as what happened with you and Dad. It wasn't as bad as that guy I used to date. The doctors said that when *that* guy hit me, I lost 80 percent of the hearing in my left ear. I'll probably never get it back.

Judith Berry: We certainly know how to pick 'em, don't we?

Halle Berry: I guess. Mom, I think it's time that I took more control of my life—at home and at work.

Scene 4

Narrator 1: Soon, Halle is trying to sell a new motion picture project of her own. It's about African American singer and actress Dorothy Dandridge. Dandridge is one of Halle's heroes. Halle wants to find someone to make the film. Then she will play the lead role herself.

Studio Boss: No, no, no. We can't do this movie. Nobody knows who this woman was!

Halle Berry: That's why the movie has to be made! You have no idea how much of a hero she was to women of color. She was a great performer. And she led such a tragic life.

Studio Boss: I'm sorry, Halle. Janet Jackson and Whitney Houston are shopping around the same project. I'll tell you what I told them: this movie will never get made.

Narrator 2: The studio boss is wrong. *Introducing Dorothy Dandridge* is made as a cable TV movie. Halle wins several awards for her performance.

Narrator 1: Soon, Hollywood begins to recognize Halle's talent. As one of her next jobs, she takes a role in the movie *X-Men*. In it, she plays a mutant superhero called "Storm." She talks to reporters.

Halle Berry: The mutants in this movie face many of the same problems that we do as African Americans. They struggle to find equality in a world of non-mutants who fear them out of ignorance. Storm reminds us that we have to teach people not to be afraid. We have to teach them not to be ignorant.

Narrator 2: Over the next few months, Halle marries her boyfriend, singer Eric Benet. She also becomes very close to Benet's eight-year-old daughter, India. India was just a toddler when her mother died.

Narrator 1: Next, Halle stars in *Monster's Ball*. The movie wins Halle her Oscar nomination.

Scene 5

Narrator 2: Back at the Oscars ceremony, Judith and Halle wait as Russell Crowe opens the envelope.

Russell Crowe: And the Oscar goes to . . . Halle Berry in *Monster's Ball*!

Narrator 1: The crowd goes wild and jumps to its feet. Halle is stunned. Judith throws her arm around her daughter. Finally, Halle stands up. She makes her way to the stage. Crowe hands her the Oscar. She takes it in her shaking hands. Halle is the first African American woman to win the Oscar for Best Actress.

Halle Berry: *(flustered)* Oh, my goodness. Oh, my. I'm sorry. It's just that this moment is so much bigger than me. It's for every nameless, faceless woman of color that now has a chance because this door tonight has been opened.

Narrator 2: The crowd cheers.

Halle Berry: I'm so honored. I want to thank my manager, Vincent. He's been with me for twelve years, and he's fought every fight. I thank my husband, who is a joy in my life. And thank you, India. I love you with all my heart. I also want to thank my mom. I love you Mom, so much. You gave me the strength to fight every single day. You gave me the strength to be who I want to be. And you gave me the courage to dream. Thank you all.

Narrator 1: The audience cheers once again. The bright spotlight follows Halle as she leaves the stage.

Cross Outs

Halle Berry

	A	B	C
1	Halle	opens	doors
2	addict	Monster's	Ball
3	for	Dorothy Dandridge	India
4	women	of	color

1. Cross out the name of Halle's hero in column B.

2. Cross out the 2 words in row 2 that are in the title that wins Halle an Oscar.

3. Cross out the word in column A for someone with a drug problem.

4. Cross out the name of Halle's stepdaughter in column C.

Write the remaining words in order below.

_____ _____ _____ _____

_____ _____ _____ .

Andrea Bocelli

Tenor

Summary

Andrea Bocelli was a toddler when he was diagnosed with glaucoma, leaving him almost blind. He went to a special school for the visually impaired, where he eventually lost all remaining vision when hit by a soccer ball. Andrea is not only intelligent, he also has an amazing singing voice. While studying law, he continued his voice training. Eventually, Bocelli got his big break, singing with Italian vocal star, Zucchero [pronounced ZOOK-ah-row]. Bocelli has become one of the world's finest tenors.

Presentation Suggestions

Students can find Italy on a map before the reading. Bring in a recording of Bocelli, and play a short piece before the reading. After the reading, discuss what it must be like to learn a whole new way of reading and writing. During the reading, have the adults sound sympathetic, but matter of fact, regarding Andrea's limitations.

Related Book and Media

- Bocelli, Andrea. *The Music of Silence: A Memoir.* New York: HarperCollins, 1999.

- http://www.andreabocelli.com

Characters

Narrator 1

Narrator 2

Mrs. Bocelli

Andrea

Doctor

Mr. Bocelli

Teacher

Lifeguard

Brother

Enrica

Andrea Bocelli
Tenor

Scene 1

Narrator 1: Mrs. Bocelli is shopping in Turin, Italy. She looks for her young son. She can't see him. Then she looks up. Andrea is on top of a short wall.

Mrs. Bocelli: Andrea! Get down from there!

Narrator 2: Andrea loves to climb. Most four-year-old kids do. But Andrea is not like most kids. He is blind in one eye. He can see only a little with the other eye.

Andrea: I'm fine! Watch me!

Mrs. Bocelli: That's not safe! Get down now! We need to finish shopping. Then we need to go to the eye doctor.

Andrea: Okay . . .

Narrator 1: Andrea is used to going to doctors. His parents hope to find a cure for his blindness. Nothing helps. But they keep trying. This doctor talks to them about school.

Doctor: I am sorry to give you bad news. Andrea is not going to get better. It is time to start thinking about school.

Mrs. Bocelli: What do you mean?

Doctor: Andrea should go to a school for the blind.

Mrs. Bocelli: But he can still see a bit.

Doctor: He can see now. But he may become blind in his other eye. We don't know what will happen. He needs to be ready for the future.

Mrs. Bocelli: What do you mean?

Doctor: He needs to learn to read Braille. A school for the blind can give him the skills he needs.

Mrs. Bocelli: I'll talk to my husband, Doctor. Thank you.

Scene 2

Narrator 2: Andrea's parents choose a boarding school. The day comes when Andrea must leave home. Mr. and Mrs. Bocelli talk with each other.

Mr. Bocelli: I don't like this idea.

Mrs. Bocelli: We have no choice. Andrea needs this school.

Mr. Bocelli: I know he needs to learn. But I want him home. I didn't like boarding school.

Mrs. Bocelli: He'll be fine. He will get used to it.

Narrator 1: Andrea's parents say goodbye at the classroom. It is his first time in school.

Teacher: Andrea, sit here. This is John. He will help you. Now, let's get started with our lessons.

Narrator 2: Andrea is smart. He learns quickly. Teachers also notice that he can sing well. At the end of third grade, he sings in his first program. He waits his turn backstage.

Andrea: Teacher, everyone is talking. Do you think they will listen to me?

Teacher: Just do your best. It will be fine.

Narrator 1: Andrea stands on stage. The people talk quietly. Then Andrea begins to sing. He sings the first few notes as loud as he can. Everyone stops talking. Everyone listens. Everyone cheers when he is done.

Teacher: See, Andrea. I told you it would be fine. You did a great job!

Scene 3

Narrator 2: Andrea likes his summers at home. His family spends part of each summer at the beach.

Mr. Bocelli: Andrea, it is time for you to learn how to swim.

Andrea: Are you going to teach me?

Mr. Bocelli: No, the lifeguard will teach you.

Mrs. Bocelli: Do you think that is a good idea?

Mr. Bocelli: Of course! Andrea is strong. He needs to be strong in the water too.

Narrator 1: The day of the lesson arrives.

Lifeguard: Let's go, Andrea. Time to learn to swim!

Andrea: What do I do?

Lifeguard: Get in the boat. We'll go out a ways. Then you can jump in.

Andrea: No. I don't want to jump in.

Lifeguard: You'll be fine. Here we are. This is a good place. Jump in.

Andrea: No.

Narrator 2: The lifeguard throws Andrea in the water. He jumps in after him.

Lifeguard: Relax, Andrea. You can do this.

Narrator 1: Soon Andrea is swimming happily. He is a good swimmer. He even wants to join the swim team.

Narrator 2: Andrea likes all kinds of sports. At the end of fifth grade, he plays soccer. One day he is the goalkeeper. He is hit by the ball. He is hit in his good eye.

Teacher: Andrea, are you okay?

Andrea: I think so. But my eye hurts.

Teacher: Let's get you to the nurse.

Narrator 1: The next day, Andrea's mother takes him to the eye doctor. The doctor tries his best. Nothing helps. Andrea is totally blind.

Scene 4

Narrator 2: Andrea and his family are sad that summer. Then they start talking about school again. Andrea wants to go to a new school. They start planning for the fall. Then Andrea hears about a music contest.

Andrea: Can I do this contest, Father? How does it work?

Mr. Bocelli: Of course you can. We will go to the café. There will be many people there. Your turn will come, and you will sing.

Andrea: Then what happens?

Mr. Bocelli: People will vote. If you win, you will go to the finals. If you win that, you get a prize.

Narrator 1: Andrea sings his best. The people vote for their favorites. Andrea wins. He wins the finals too. Andrea dreams of being a fine singer.

Narrator 2: But Andrea is still young. First he has to go to school. His parents expect him to study hard. For many years he does study hard. He also falls in love. He falls in love a lot!

Narrator 1: He sings a lot, too. He dreams of becoming a lawyer. He knows that dream can come true. He also dreams of finding a girlfriend. That dream doesn't always work out. He dates. But nothing works for long.

Narrator 2: But his big dream is to be a singer. Andrea sings at weddings. He sings in clubs. Sometimes his brother goes with him. One night they are in a club.

Brother: Andrea, a girl wants to meet you.

Andrea: What girl?

Brother: Her name is Enrica. Her friend is Cara. They want to talk with us at the break.

Andrea: Why not?

Narrator 1: The young people have a good time. Andrea thinks Enrica is special. She might be the one for him.

Scene 5

Narrator 2: Andrea keeps taking singing lessons. By now he is in his twenties. One day he gets a phone call from a recording studio. He still dreams of being a famous singer. His dream might just come true!

Andrea: Father! Mother! I have been asked to sing for a record! It's a duet. If they like me I will get a contract.

Mr. Bocelli: Who will you sing with?

Andrea: With Zucchero!

Mrs. Bocelli: That is grand! He is such a famous singer! But he is not an opera singer.

Andrea: I know. They want this to be an unusual duet. This is my break. I just know it!

Narrator 1: Andrea sings well at the studio. The people there say someone will call him. He waits for the phone to ring with the news. But no one calls.

Narrator 2: Andrea has other things to think about. He and Enrica are in love. They are going to be married. He is filled with joy at their wedding. Soon after he finds out he won't be singing with Zucchero. He is sad for months. Then the phone rings again. This time the news is very good.

Andrea: Enrica, I have news!

Enrica: What is it?

Andrea: Zucchero wants me to sing with him!

Enrica: On a recording?

Andrea: Not this time! It will be on stage. There is a big concert. There is a concert tour. This is my chance!

Enrica: Let's call your parents!

Scene 6

Narrator 1: Andrea stands backstage. There are 15,000 people in the audience. He thinks about the first time he sang in front of people.

Andrea: (*to himself*) I wonder if people will listen to me this time? Will they like me? I don't sing like Zucchero.

Narrator 2: The time for the duet comes. Andrea goes onstage. He sits at a piano. He sings his first notes. The audience starts to cheer. Andrea keeps singing. Soon the concert is over. The audience cheers and cheers! Enrica and his family greet him.

Enrica: You were wonderful!

Mrs. Bocelli: Did you hear the audience? They loved you!

Mr. Bocelli: Andrea, I am so proud of you!

Andrea: Thank you. Thank you. I feel like I'm in a dream . . .

Narrator 1: Andrea's dreams do come true. That first tour was a great success. He went on to become a famous singer. He cannot see—but his singing brings joy to all who hear him.

Cross Outs

Andrea Bocelli

	A	B	C
1	law	singing	Mr. Bocelli
2	is	blindness	Mrs. Bocelli
3	Braille	lifeguard	Andrea's
4	biggest	dream	Enrica

1. Cross out two things that Andrea studied in column A.
2. Cross out what Andrea overcame in column B.
3. Cross out three names of Andrea's family in column C.
4. Cross out the person who taught Andrea to swim in row 3.

Write the remaining words in order below.

_____   _____   _____   _____

_____.

Diana Golden Brosnihan

Skier

Summary

At age twelve, Diana Golden lost her leg to cancer. An avid skier, she learned to ski again and joined the U.S. Disabled Ski Team from 1979 to 1982. After college, she joined the team again, from 1985 to 1990. This script describes her repeated struggles with cancer, her despair and suicide attempts, and how she found love with Steve Brosnihan just four years before dying at age thirty-eight. Diana won numerous medals as a disabled skier and was honored as an outstanding athlete. She was named Skier of the Year by *Skiing Magazine* and the U.S. Olympic Committee. She won the Flo Hyman Award from the Women's Sports Foundation in 1991. In 1997 she was inducted into the U.S. National Ski Hall of Fame and the International Women's Sports Hall of Fame.

Presentation Suggestions

Skiing equipment can be used as props. Posters or murals of famous ski areas or of the mountains can serve as backdrops.

Related Book and Media

- Kaminsky, Marty. *Uncommon Champions: Fifteen Athletes Who Battled Back.* Honesdale, PA: Boyds Mills Press, 2000.

- Disabled Sports USA: www.dsusa.org

Characters

Narrator 1

Narrator 2

Diana Golden

Mark Golden, *Diana's brother*

Meryl Golden, *Diana's sister*

Doctor 1

Mrs. Golden, *Diana's mother*

Kirk Bauer, *teacher*

Steve Brosnihan, *Diana's husband*

Doctor 2

Diana Golden Brosnihan
Skier

Scene 1

Narrator 1: Diana races down the ski slopes. She is skiing with her brother and sister. Diana is already a great skier at age twelve. This is their last run of the day.

Diana Golden: What a great day!

Mark Golden: Too bad we have to quit.

Meryl Golden: Let's be here when the lifts start running in the morning.

Diana Golden: Sounds good to me!

Narrator 2: A few days later Diana is walking in the snow near their house in New Hampshire. Diana falls down suddenly.

Diana Golden: Ouch!

Mark Golden: Are you okay?

Diana Golden: Yeah. My knee just gave out.

Meryl Golden: That's odd. Maybe you're just tired.

Diana Golden: Yeah. No big deal.

Narrator 2: Diana's leg keeps giving her trouble. She goes to some doctors. One doctor runs some tests. He finds out that she has cancer. Diana and her parents meet with the doctor to talk about the results.

Diana Golden: Doctor, have you found out what's wrong?

Doctor 1: Yes. But I don't have good news.

Diana Golden: What is it?

Doctor 1: You have bone cancer.

Mrs. Golden: Cancer! How can you treat it?

Doctor 1: In this case there is only one option. We have to remove the leg.

Mrs. Golden: You want to take her leg?

Doctor 1: That's best.

Diana Golden: How much of my leg will I lose?

Doctor 1: We need to take it above the knee.

Diana Golden: Will I still be able to ski?

Doctor 1: Of course. You will have to learn how again. But lots of people who lose an arm or a leg do great.

Diana Golden: Well, let's get it done then.

Scene 2

Narrator 1: Diana goes to a ski class after having her leg removed. She meets Kirk Bauer. He will teach her how to ski again.

Kirk Bauer: Hi, Diana. Are you ready to tear down the slopes?

Diana Golden: I doubt if I'll be tearing down the slopes for a long time.

Kirk Bauer: You might be surprised. I hear you were a fine skier before you got cancer.

Diana Golden: But I had two legs then.

Kirk Bauer: You will have to learn some new ways of skiing. It's up to you. Do you want to ski again?

Diana Golden: I suppose.

Kirk Bauer: Are you sure?

Diana Golden: Yes!

Kirk Bauer: Then let's get to work.

Narrator 2: Diana is small and skinny. But she is a gifted athlete. She also learns to work hard. One day Kirk talks with Diana's mother about her progress.

Mrs. Golden: How is Diana doing, Kirk?

Kirk Bauer: She's getting better by the day.

Mrs. Golden: I worry about her. I don't want her to quit. She seems to need this.

Kirk Bauer: I agree that she needs this. She's a smart kid. She has a lot of energy. If she doesn't use the energy to ski, I'm afraid she'll get into a lot of trouble.

Mrs. Golden: She is strong-minded.

Kirk Bauer: *(laughing)* That's putting it mildly! I'd like to get her competing as soon as she can. I think she can win races if she puts her mind to it. Is that okay with you?

Mrs. Golden: Of course! Let's do whatever it takes. She'll feel a lot better about herself once she's doing well on the slopes.

Narrator 1: Diana works hard at skiing. She begins to win races. She talks with her brother and sister after a race.

Meryl Golden: You were great out there today, Diana.

Mark Golden: No one could touch you!

Diana Golden: It felt good! You know what I like about these races?

Meryl Golden: Winning?

Mark Golden: The TV cameras? The fans?

Diana Golden: Well, I was going to say I like winning. But you're right, Mark. I love the attention. I'd love to ski full time—and keep getting better.

Scene 3

Narrator 2: Diana keeps skiing and winning. She goes to college. That takes all her energy for a while, forcing her to take a break from skiing. Then she goes back to skiing and racing. She wins nineteen U.S. and ten world disabled gold medals.

Narrator 1: Diana is admired for being more than a disabled athlete. She's honored for being a world-class athlete. She competes until 1991. Then she decides to quit skiing. She starts giving speeches. Her motto is "Yes I Can!" She tells people to try hard like she does.

Narrator 2: In late 1992 Diana finds a lump in her breast. She goes to a doctor who gives her the bad news.

Doctor 2: Diana, you have breast cancer.

Diana Golden: Well, I've been through it before. What do I have to do this time?

Doctor 2: You'll need chemotherapy. And we should remove the breast.

Narrator 1: A week later Diana meets with the doctor again.

Doctor 2: I want to check out your other breast. There are some spots on it. It's probably nothing. But let's be safe.

Narrator 2: Diana gets more bad news. Both breasts must be removed. Diana bravely goes through the surgery. Then her doctors find a growth on her uterus. They have to remove it. Now Diana can never have children. Her family tries to comfort her.

Mark Golden: Diana, you're going to be fine. You'll find a way to have a full life.

Meryl Golden: You're a winner, after all.

Diana Golden: I don't feel like much of a winner. I'm sick of being sick. The chemo is rough. I'm weak all the time.

Meryl Golden: But this is what will make you better. You have to stick it out.

Mark Golden: You've done it before, kid.

Diana Golden: I know, but this time.. . . I don't know about this time. I really wanted to have children.

Meryl Golden: It will get better. Just keep fighting.

Narrator 1: Diana wants to believe it will get better. But she gets tired of fighting. She can't say "Yes I can" anymore. She wants to give up.

Narrator 2: In 1993 she almost gives up forever. She takes an overdose of pills. Just in time, she changes her mind. She calls a friend. She is rushed to the hospital.

Narrator 1: Diana tries to deal with her cancer. She writes about her feelings. She gets a puppy. After just a month the puppy dies. Once again, she decides to kill herself. She plans to jump into a canyon in Colorado.

Narrator 2: Instead, she calls a crisis center. She gets help. Diana begins to fight back. She gets a new puppy. She calls him Midnight Sun. He becomes her "light in the night." She starts the next round in her fight.

Scene 4

Narrator 1: In 1996, Diana gets bad news again. She has learned that the cancer has spread to her skeletal system. She wonders how she'll keep going. Her friends push her to go to a Halloween party. A man in a bug suit sees her across the room.

Steve: Diana?

Diana Golden: Yes.

Steve: We know each other.

Diana Golden: We do?

Steve: Yes. We went to school together. My name is Steve.

Diana Golden: Steve?

Steve: Yes.

Narrator 2: Steve remembers Diana from college. He didn't know her then. But he always liked her bright smile. He decides he wants to get to know her. They start to date.

Narrator 1: Diana decides she has to be very open with Steve.

Diana Golden: Steve, we need to talk.

Steve: What about?

Diana Golden: You know I've had cancer.

Steve: Of course. So?

Diana Golden: I've lost my leg. I've lost both breasts. I've lost my uterus.

Narrator 2: Steve knows she has more to say.

Diana Golden: The cancer is spreading. I am still getting chemo. My chances aren't good.

Steve: That doesn't scare me, Diana.

Diana Golden: It scares me, Steve. I don't want to get involved with you and then have things go wrong. I couldn't stand it.

Steve: Diana, don't worry. I'm not going anywhere.

Narrator 1: Steve means what he says. He's in love with Diana. She falls in love with him. One day she is shopping with her sister. She sees a white dress.

Diana Golden: I'm going to buy that dress for my wedding!

Meryl Golden: Your wedding? Don't you think you should wait until Steve proposes?

Diana Golden: Oh, he will. He will.

Narrator 2: Diana buys the dress. Steve knows that chemo days are rough. So he proposes on a chemo day. It's also Valentine's Day in 1997. Diana says yes.

Narrator 1: Diana and Steve get married on August 9, 1997. She wears the white dress she bought with her sister. Diana and Steve promise to love each other forever. They look forward to the life they will have together.

Epilogue, Diana Golden Brosnihan

Narrator 2: Diana and Steve enjoy married life. Diana keeps fighting the cancer. During her speeches she would say, "When we fail, we have to get up again and again."

Narrator 1: Diana keeps getting back up to fight for four years. She dies on August 26, 2001.

Cross Outs

Diana Golden Brosnihan

	A	B	C
1	winning	attention	say
2	Midnight Sun	yes	I
3	can	crisis center	Mark
4	to	life	Meryl

1. Cross out the name of Diana's puppy in column A.

2. Cross out the 2 words in row 1 that tell what Diana liked about racing.

3. Cross out the names of Diana's brother and sister in column C.

4. Cross out the name of a place to get help in column B.

Write the remaining words in order below.

_____   _____   _____   _____

_____   _____.

Tedy Bruschi

Football Player

Summary

Tedy Bruschi is a star linebacker for the New England Patriots. In 2005, at age thirty-one, Bruschi suffered a stroke that threatened not just his pro football career, but his life.

This play tells the story of Bruschi's sudden, shocking illness and how he defied all odds and returned to professional football the following season. At the time of this writing, Bruschi not only continues to anchor the Patriots' defense, he also devotes himself to raising awareness about strokes, America's number one disabler and number three killer.

Presentation Suggestions

Before reading the play, students might familiarize themselves with Bruschi's rough-and-tumble line of work by watching highlights of a pro football game. Someone familiar with football might explain to the class what a linebacker does and the physical and intellectual demands the position places on the player. A linebacker from a local high school or college football team could talk about playing the position and the players whom the guest speaker emulates.

Related Book and Media

- Bruschi, Tedy, and Michael Holley. *Never Give Up: My Stroke, My Recovery, and My Return to the NFL.* Hoboken, NJ: John Wiley & Sons, 2007.

- American Stroke Association: www.strokeassociation.org; see "Tedy's Team."

Characters

Talk Show Host

Tedy Bruschi, *a professional football player*

Heidi Bruschi, *Tedy's wife*

TJ Bruschi, *Tedy and Heidi's son*

Doctor

Therapist

Announcer

 **Tedy Bruschi**
Football Player

Scene 1

Talk Show Host: Good afternoon, fans, and welcome to another afternoon of *Sports Talk Live.* Today, we have a very special guest on the line—Tedy Bruschi, star linebacker of the New England Patriots. Welcome to the show, Tedy.

Tedy Bruschi: Thanks. It's a pleasure to speak with you.

Host: This is a very special day for Tedy, because we've just learned that he's been named the Associated Press Comeback Player of the Year. How does this award make you feel?

Tedy Bruschi: Well, it's a great honor. And it's a little bit overwhelming. I've only been out of action for about a year. But at the same time, it's been a long, long road back.

Host: Tell us about what you've been through, Tedy. Tell us the story from the beginning.

Tedy Bruschi: Sure. It started in February 2005. I was on top of the world. It was only a couple of weeks after the Patriots won our second championship in a row. It was our third in four years. I had just returned from Hawaii. I played in my first Pro Bowl, the all-star game for football players. I had a beautiful wife, three great sons. In fact, my third son had just been born a few weeks before. I had everything I could have ever hoped for. But my life would change suddenly, in the middle of the night . . .

Scene 2

Heidi Bruschi: *(half asleep)* Tedy? Are you all right?

Tedy Bruschi: Yeah . . . I just . . . I have to go to the bathroom . . .

Heidi Bruschi: So what's wrong?

Tedy Bruschi: My arm and leg . . . they're numb etc. and I have a really bad headache . . .

Heidi Bruschi: Why? What happened?

Tedy Bruschi: I don't know. It must have been the game. I must have taken a bad hit . . . or slept funny on my side.

Heidi Bruschi: Do you need help?

Tedy Bruschi: No . . . I can make it . . .

Heidi Bruschi: *(going back to sleep)* Okay . . .

Tedy Bruschi: But I wasn't okay. I could barely make it to the bathroom and back. I collapsed on the bed and slept for a few more hours. When I woke up, the numbness was still there. And so was the headache.

Heidi Bruschi: Does it still hurt?

Tedy Bruschi: It's awful. It's the worst headache I've ever had . . .

Heidi Bruschi: My father's a physician's assistant. Let me call him and see what he thinks.

TJ Bruschi: *(entering the room)* Hi, Mommy! Hi, Daddy!

Heidi Bruschi: Hello, sweetheart.

Tedy Bruschi: TJ? Where are you?

TJ Bruschi: *(stepping in front of his father)* I'm right here!

Tedy Bruschi: Oh—there you are. Uh . . . hey, buddy! How are you?

TJ Bruschi: What's wrong, Daddy? Did I scare you?

Tedy Bruschi: Um . . . no, TJ. Of course not. Listen, why don't you go downstairs. We'll come down in a minute to make you breakfast.

TJ Bruschi: Okay!

Heidi Bruschi: Tedy, what's the matter?

Tedy Bruschi: I couldn't see him, Heidi. I couldn't see him walk up to me. I didn't see him until he was right in front of me.

Heidi Bruschi: *(terrified)* Tedy . . .

Tedy Bruschi: Call 911. Quick.

Scene 3

Tedy Bruschi: The ambulance came. I was rushed to the hospital. They did a whole bunch of tests on me. Finally, the doctor came in to talk to us.

Doctor: Tedy, I've looked at all the results. I'm afraid you've had a stroke.

Heidi Bruschi: Oh, no!

Tedy Bruschi: That's impossible!

Doctor: I'm afraid not. You see, Tedy, a stroke is when there's an interruption of blood flow to the brain. We think in your case, the cause was a small hole in your heart.

Heidi Bruschi: Tedy has a hole in his heart?

Doctor: Actually, it's something all babies are born with. For most people, the hole closes as they grow. For about 20 percent of the population, though, the hole stays open.

Tedy Bruschi: But how did that cause a stroke?

Doctor: We think a blood clot formed somewhere in your body. The hole let the clot pass through your heart and to your brain.

Heidi Bruschi: *(in tears)* Oh, no . . .

Tedy Bruschi: Doctor . . . how bad is it?

Doctor: We're going to have to do more tests on you. We will watch you closely over the next two weeks. We need to find out how bad the damage is. And we need to make sure that another stroke doesn't happen. Then we're going to have to talk about surgery. We need to close the hole in your heart.

Talk Show Host: Tedy, were you even thinking about football at that time?

Tedy Bruschi: Not at first. I was thinking about getting my normal body function back. And I was thinking about just being a husband and a father. Even when I got out of the hospital, I still wasn't back to normal. And that's when it began to set in . . .

Heidi Bruschi: Okay, Tedy—are you all set?

Tedy Bruschi: Well, I can't walk right. I still can't see out of my left eye. Other than that, I'm great.

Heidi Bruschi: Tedy, consider yourself lucky. Remember what the doctor said. You could have died.

Tedy Bruschi: I know. And yes, I know I'm lucky. But . . . football has been part of my life since I was fourteen years old. And now it's over. I'm done. I'll never play again.

Heidi Bruschi: So you'll do something else with your life. And I'll be there with you, and so will the boys.

Tedy Bruschi: All right. Let's go home.

Heidi Bruschi: Okay. Now remember, there's going to be a lot of reporters out there. Just relax and take your time. The car is right at the end of the sidewalk.

Tedy Bruschi: Right. Hold on tight to my arm. And . . . honey?

Heidi Bruschi: Yes?

Tedy Bruschi: Please . . . don't let me fall.

Scene 4

Talk Show Host: What happened then, Tedy?

Tedy Bruschi: I worked to get better. I had the surgery to fix the hole in my heart. I took my medicine. Slowly, my vision returned. I worked hard. Over time, my body began to return to normal.

Therapist: All right, Tedy, you've been able to catch the ball. Now I want you to do it while standing on the balance beam.

Tedy Bruschi: No problem. Go ahead, toss it over.

Therapist: *(throwing the ball)* Excellent! Now, can you throw and catch it while walking down the beam?

Tedy Bruschi: That shouldn't be too hard . . .

Therapist: Tedy, you've had to learn how to walk all over again. You've been making great progress.

Tedy Bruschi: It helps when you have a goal to shoot for.

Therapist: What kind of goal?

Tedy Bruschi: I've been thinking . . . I want to play football again. Do you think I can?

Therapist: As far as I can tell, you are fine. You'll have to talk to your doctors, of course. But I don't see any reason why not.

Talk Show Host: What did your wife think of your plans, Tedy?

Tedy Bruschi: Well . . . let's just say that she wasn't sure.

Heidi Bruschi: No. No! Tedy, you can't be serious!

Tedy Bruschi: I'm totally serious. Honey, a normal life after a stroke is going back to work. This is my work. I just want my normal life back.

Heidi Bruschi: I can't let you do this! What about the children?

Tedy Bruschi: I want to teach our kids something. They can face—and beat—a challenge. How can I do that if I don't try?

Heidi Bruschi: But . . . what if something happens to you?

Tedy Bruschi: We'll check with the doctors. And I won't do it without their go-ahead.

Heidi Bruschi: Well . . . all right. If you're going to do it, you're not going to do it alone. I'm with you. We'll do this together.

Scene 5

Announcer: And now it's third down and five yards to go for Buffalo. The game could ride on this play! There's the snap—the quarterback hands off the ball. The running back is tackled for a loss by Tedy Bruschi! That's ten tackles for Bruschi. The Patriots are going to win the game! What a game! Tedy Bruschi was great!

Talk Show Host: You were named the AFC Defensive Player of the Week. And this was after your first game back, Tedy. That must have been quite a thrill.

Tedy Bruschi: It sure was. I was pretty nervous before that game. And there was one play early on when a couple of 300-pound guys piled on me. I got up and thought, "Hey, I'm still alive!" We didn't make it to the Super Bowl. But I know our best days are still ahead of us.

Talk Show Host: And what about you, Tedy? Are your best days still ahead of you?

Tedy Bruschi: Absolutely. I have a cause now. About 700,000 people in America have strokes each year. And a lot of them aren't as lucky as I was. People should know the symptoms of stroke: headaches, numbness on one side, dizziness, loss of balance, and slurring of words. If this happens, people should get help fast. That helps their chances of getting well again.

Talk Show Host: Tedy, thanks for giving us a few minutes of your time. Best of luck in the future.

Tedy Bruschi: Thank you. I've already had a lot of luck. With that, and some hard work, you can make anything happen.

Cross Outs

Tedy Bruschi

	A	B	C
1	touchdown	champions	tackles
2	never	medicine	coach
3	grass	give	run
4	band	kick	up

1. Cross out the word for a scoring play in football in row 1.

2. Cross out the word for what a linebacker does to someone holding a football in column C.

3. Cross out the word for what covers a football field in row 3.

4. Cross out the word for the person who runs the football team in column C.

5. Cross out the word for the people who play music at a football game in column A.

6. Cross out the word for what people take when they're sick in column B.

7. Cross out the word in row 4 for what happens when you strike the ball with your foot.

8. Cross out the word in column C for what you want to do when you're holding the ball.

Write the remaining words in order below.

_____ _____ _____ _____ .

Tom Cruise

Actor

Summary

Most people knew Tom Cruise Mapother IV as a youngster with reading problems. Born July 3, 1962, Tom was eleven years old when his parents divorced. His mother moved the family regularly during Tom's school years, searching for work. The family was poor, which led to his mother getting him a scholarship to a Catholic Seminary. Tom benefited from the discipline and smaller classes and briefly considered becoming a priest. He coped with feeling inadequate scholastically by participating in sports. After a wrestling injury, he tried out for a school musical. This lead to his decision to take ten years to try to make it in show business. Within a year, he had landed his first film.

Presentation Suggestions

Students can research the styles and dress appropriately for the '70s. Students can decorate the stage with movie posters of films in which Cruise appeared. Tom should sit with his mother and sisters next to him. The narrators and other cast members can stand to the side.

Related Books

• Wheeler, Jill C. *Tom Cruise.* Edina, MN: Abdo and Daughters, 2002.

• Sellers, Robert. *Tom Cruise: A Biography.* New York: Robert Hale, 2000.

Characters

Narrator 1

Narrator 2

Father

Tom Cruise

Mother

Teacher

Marian Cruise, *Tom's sister*

Lee Anne Cruise, *Tom's sister*

Cass Cruise, *Tom's sister*

Mr. Lewis, *Tom's neighbor*

Jack South, *Tom's stepfather*

 # Tom Cruise
Actor

Scene 1

Narrator 1: Tom sits quietly with his sisters. Tom is eleven years old. He can't believe what his parents are saying.

Father: I know divorce is hard to understand. But your mother and I haven't been happy together for a long time.

Tom Cruise: But what about us? Who's going to take care of us?

Mother: You'll be with me, of course.

Marian Cruise: Will we have to move?

Mother: I hope not. I'll have to get a job. We'll all have to pull together. I'll be counting on you all.

Father: You know that we both love you very much. This isn't about you. It's about your mother and me.

Lee Anne Cruise: Will we stay here?

Mother: We haven't figured out everything yet. You don't need to worry.

Narrator 2: Later, Tom talks with his sisters.

Tom Cruise: I don't understand why they couldn't stay together. We need our dad.

Cass Cruise: You know Mom will take good care of us. If she gets a good job maybe we can get a house.

Marian Cruise: Wouldn't it be nice to stay in one place? The longest we've ever lived anywhere is two years.

Tom Cruise: I hate changing schools so much. I don't think I'll ever catch up to the other kids. I always feel so stupid.

Lee Anne Cruise: You aren't stupid, Tom. You just have trouble reading. You just have to keep trying.

Tom Cruise: You don't know what it's like. The kids tease me. I never get a chance to make friends. I'm always the new kid. Worse yet, I'm the new kid who can't read.

Cass Cruise: Well, we can't do anything about this. We might as well make the best of it.

Scene 2

Narrator 1: It is early in the morning. Mrs. Mapother loads the kids and a few belongings into a car. They drive away from a small town near Ottawa, Canada.

Narrator 2: Mrs. Mapother doesn't have much money. She has to take the family to where she grew up in Louisville, Kentucky.

Mother: Don't worry kids. My family will help us get set up. It will be a lot better.

Narrator 1: Soon the family is settled. Mrs. Mapother has a job. Tom and his sisters discuss their first day at the new school. Their mother listens.

Cass Cruise: How was school, Tom?

Tom Cruise: It was about like always.

Marian Cruise: What do you mean?

Tom Cruise: I'm behind the other kids.

Mother: I had trouble learning to read, Tom. I'll help you.

Lee Anne Cruise: Can't the teachers help?

Tom Cruise: There are so many kids. I don't think they have the time. Besides, I don't like kids to know I can't read much.

Cass Cruise: Are there any sports you can go out for? Some junior highs have football and basketball.

Marian Cruise: That's a good idea. You're a good athlete, Tom.

Tom Cruise: I might do that.

Narrator 2: Tom decides to go out for basketball. He finds out that he's pretty good. He meets other kids and makes a few friends.

Scene 3

Narrator 1: The family never has much money. But Mrs. Mapother manages to put food on the table. The family keeps moving so she can get jobs. Now they live in Ohio.

Narrator 2: It's almost time for Tom to start his freshman year. Mrs. Mapother brings the family together.

Mother: Tom, girls. I've made a hard decision. We are barely getting by. I don't have enough money for school clothes. It will be hard to feed everyone.

Marian Cruise: What are we going to do, Mom? We all have jobs.

Mother: I know. You're all great. Each of you helps out so much. There is a way to make things easier for us to get by. But it won't be easier for you, Tom.

Tom Cruise: What do you mean?

Mother: There's a Catholic school near Cincinnati. They've agreed to let you attend. They'll give you clothes, feed you well, and give you a good education. Their classes are small. I think you'll get more help with your reading problem.

Tom Cruise: It sounds like you have it all arranged.

Mother: I'm sorry, Son. I hope this only lasts a year.

Narrator 1: Tom finds that the school gives his life some order. He begins to like the school.

Narrator 2: Later, Tom talks about school with Bill Lewis. Bill lives next door to the family. Tom did odd jobs for him.

Mr. Lewis: How is school, Tom?

Tom Cruise: I didn't think I'd like it. But the classes are small. I'm getting lots of help.

Mr. Lewis: That's good, Tom. Are they really strict?

Tom Cruise: They sure are! The priests and the nuns don't let you get away with anything! You can't even skip a stair without getting into trouble.

Mr. Lewis: What about going to mass? How's that?

Tom Cruise: I like that. In fact I'm thinking about becoming a priest.

Mr. Lewis: Really? That can be a good life. You could help a lot of people. Have you thought about it a lot?

Tom Cruise: Well, I'm just starting to.

Mr. Lewis: I think you'll be good at whatever you decide to do. Just think about what will make you happy.

Tom Cruise: I'll keep thinking about it.

Narrator 1: But Tom doesn't think too long about becoming a priest. He and some friends sneak out to see some girls one weekend. Before long, Tom decides he would rather get to know girls than become a priest!

Scene 4

Narrator 2: When Tom is sixteen, his mom tells the family that she plans to marry Jack South. Tom wants his mother to be happy. But he has enjoyed being the head of the family. He's not sure he wants a stepfather. Then he gets worse news.

Jack South: Tom, girls, sit down.

Lee Anne Cruise: What's going on?

Jack South: Your mother and I have decided to move.

Lee Anne Cruise: Where to?

Jack South: To a nice town in New Jersey.

Tom Cruise: New Jersey! I don't want to change schools now! I'm about to start my senior year.

Jack South: I know it's tough. But you'll be able to play football. I hear they have a good wrestling team, too. We'll be able to get a nice house there.

Narrator 1: Tom and his sisters see they have no choice. Tom plays football, but gets thrown off the team for drinking alcohol. Tom is a natural at wrestling.

Narrator 2: He joins the team and hopes to win a college scholarship. One night he is exercising before a meet. He runs up the stairs and trips. He falls a whole flight of stairs and hurts himself. His wrestling season is over.

Narrator 1: A teacher has another idea for him. This idea changes his life.

Teacher: Tom, you're a pretty good singer. Why don't you try out for the school's musical?

Tom Cruise: What's the musical?

Teacher: It's called *Guys and Dolls.*

Tom Cruise: I might as well. I can't wrestle anymore.

Narrator 2: Tom gets to play a big role. He does a great job. Now he knows what he wants to do. He talks it over with his mother and Jack.

Tom Cruise: Mom, Jack. After the show an agent talked to me. He said I should try being an actor. I want to try it.

Mother: Tom, this is a big decision. You are talented. But it's tough to break in.

Jack South: Are you sure this is what you want to do?

Tom Cruise: I've given it a lot of thought. I still don't read well enough to go to college. I've saved up some money.

Jack South: Maybe you should learn a trade first. You know, something you can fall back on.

Tom Cruise: I know I can do this. I just want your blessing.

Mother: Tom, if you believe you can do that, so do I.

Jack South: We only want the best for you.

Narrator 1: Tom is just seventeen when he goes to New York City in 1980. He waits tables and unloads trucks to earn money. He takes acting classes and goes to auditions. He drops his last name. He is now known as Tom Cruise.

Narrator 2: In 1981 Tom Cruise appears in *Endless Love,* his first film. The film flops. But Tom's next films are much better. His roles in *Taps* and *The Outsiders* set Tom Cruise on a journey that few actors have achieved.

Narrator 1: The young man who struggled to read is now one of the most successful actors in the world.

 **Cross Outs**

Tom Cruise

	A	B	C
1	Cass	Tom	waits tables
2	cruises	to	wrestling
3	Marian	acting	success
4	Lee Anne	*Endless Love*	football

1. Cross out the 2 sports Tom tries in column C.

2. Cross out what Tom does to earn money in row 1.

3. Cross out Tom's first film in row 4.

4. Cross out the names of Tom's three sisters in column A.

Write the remaining words in order below.

_____ _____ _____ _____

_____.

Vin Diesel

Actor and Writer

Summary

In this play within a play, five students decide to research why Vin Diesel is on their teacher's list of people who have overcome odds to become successful and famous. Vin Diesel, actor and writer, grew up in the Westbeth Artists Housing complex in New York City's Greenwich Village. Claiming to be racially mixed, Vin never met his biological father and was raised by his mother and stepfather. Although his parents had limited means, they valued movies and theatre. Irving Vincent, a theater director and teacher, encouraged his son to pursue his dream of being a film star.

Presentation Suggestions

Students can have movie posters or photographs of Vin Diesel on stage. Another option is to create a scene that resembles an apartment's kitchen or living room, decorated with props such as *Star Wars* toys, model cars, and skateboards.

Related Book

- Robin, Michael. *Vin Diesel XXXposed.* New York: Pocket Books, 2002.

Characters

Narrator

Miss Perez, *teacher*

Maria, *student*

Tran, *student*

Ian, *student*

Taneka, *student*

Will, *student*

Jed, *student*

Vin Diesel
Actor and Writer

Scene 1

Narrator: Miss Perez is teaching her eighth-grade language arts class.

Miss Perez: For your final grade, you will be writing a profile about a famous and successful person. You can work in small groups. If you do work in a group I will expect a longer report.

Narrator: The class groans.

Miss Perez: There is something else. Your report has to be on someone who had to overcome something.

Maria: What do you mean, Miss Perez?

Miss Perez: Well, some people are famous because they are beautiful. Some are successful because they were born rich. Others had tough things happen in their lives. They still became successful and famous.

Maria: Can you give us some examples?

Miss Perez: Sure. Did you know that Thomas Edison, Winston Churchill, and Alexander Graham Bell had learning disabilities?

Tran: Those guys are famous. But they're all dead! I want to read about people who are alive!

Miss Perez: There are plenty of famous people who are still alive who struggled in school. People like Tom Cruise, Magic Johnson, Whoopi Goldberg, and Henry Winkler.

Tran: But those guys are old! What about someone young?

Miss Perez: What about someone like Vin Diesel? Is that someone you'd be interested in?

Maria: Did he have trouble in school?

Miss Perez: No, but he did have other kinds of challenges.

Ian: What kind?

Miss Perez: Well, I think that's something that a group of you should try to find out. I have a list of people to choose from for your reports. You can also find someone not on the list. I'll pass out the list. Start forming your groups. By the way, try to do something creative. You'll earn extra points.

Scene 2

Narrator: Ian, Will, Jed, Maria, and Taneka decide to research Vin Diesel. They meet at Will's house after school to plan.

Taneka: How are we going to do this?

Will: First we need to find out why he was on the list. Does anyone know?

Ian: I found a few things on a Web site. He grew up pretty poor in New York City. He lived in a housing complex. It was for families of artists.

Jed: I read that he didn't fit in with any one group.

Taneka: What do you mean?

Jed: He won't talk much about his race. But he seems to be a mix of lots of races. I read his dad wasn't around either. He was raised by his mom and stepdad.

Maria: Let's see. He grew up poor. His dad was gone. He is a mix of races. I can see why Miss Perez put him on the list.

Taneka: We need more than that for a report.

Will: I know we do. We also need to decide how to give the report. Most reports are so boring. And Miss Perez said we'd get extra points for being creative.

Jed: Well, why not take our cue from Vin Diesel?

Ian: What do you mean?

Jed: He's an actor. Let's act out his life.

Taneka: That's a great idea!

Will: You're right! It should be fun, too.

Ian: Well, I guess we have only one thing left to do tonight.

Maria: What's that?

Ian: Get to the library!

Scene 3

Narrator: Two weeks later Maria announces the group's report to the class.

Maria: Our report is on Vin Diesel. For our report we are going to do something we thought he'd like. We're going to read a script about his life. Ian will play Vin, whose name was Mark Vincent when he was young. Will plays his brother, Paul. Jed plays his father, Irving Vincent. Taneka is Vin's mother, Delora Vincent. And I'm the narrator.

Narrator: The students take their places in front of the class. Maria begins to read.

Act 1

Maria (Narrator): The day is July 18, 1977. The place is Greenwich Village in New York City. Mark and Paul Vincent are twins. Today is their tenth birthday. Their stepdad calls to them.

Jed (Irving): Let's go, Mark and Paul. We don't want to miss the movie.

Will (Paul): I can't believe we're finally going to see *Star Wars*.

Ian (Mark/Vin): All the guys say it's really cool.

Taneka (Delora): I hope it's good. It will be great to get out of the heat anyway.

Will (Paul): Can we have popcorn?

Jed (Irving): Well, you'll have to make a choice. It's popcorn now or Chinese food later. What's your choice?

Will (Paul): I vote for Chinese food later! What about you, Mark?

Ian (Mark/Vin): That's fine with me. We can sneak in some snacks.

Jed (Irving): Then let's go. I hear the lines are long. We don't want to miss the opening.

Maria (Narrator): After the movie, the family eats Chinese food in a restaurant on 42nd Street.

Jed (Irving): What did you think, boys? Was it as good as you expected?

Will (Paul): The special effects were great! But I thought it was slow in spots.

Ian (Mark/Vin): Darth Vader was cool. But I would have made a better Luke Skywalker.

Will (Paul): You? I doubt that!

Taneka (Delora): Well, you never know, Paul. After all, you two have been acting for a few years now.

Jed (Irving): Acting up, I'd say.. . . I still can't believe Crystal Field didn't throw you out when you sneaked into the Theater for the New City.

Ian (Mark/Vin): She told us we'd have more fun acting in the theater than trashing it.

Will (Paul): She was right. The best part was that we got paid! But, Mark. You, in a movie? Get real.

Ian (Mark/Vin): Well, just wait and see. Someday I'll be in a movie. Dad, do you think we can go to a Broadway show next week?

Jed (Irving): We won't be able to afford a Broadway show. Maybe we can see one of the off-Broadway shows next month. Let's see how the money holds up. For now, let's get home. I think there's a birthday cake and ice cream somewhere in the apartment!

Act 2

Maria (Narrator): Paul and Mark are lucky to get through their teen years. They like to run around the city on roller-blades. They grab on to buses and taxis. They are a mix of races and so don't fit in with any one group. Mark turns thirteen, and his voice gets very deep. Kids tease him. He begins bodybuilding to build his confidence. In 1985 he becomes a bouncer at a nightclub because he wants to make money. He also changes his name to Vin Diesel. He talks about his job with his dad and brother.

Jed (Irving): Son, how is the job going?

Ian (Mark/Vin): Fine, Dad. There are a lot of celebrities at the club.

Will (Paul): Do you ever get to talk with any of them?

Ian (Mark/Vin): Nothing except to say "hey." I have to keep things under control, you know. I've seen people get shot and stabbed. It can get rough.

Will (Paul): Well, don't tell your mother that! She'll make you quit.

Ian (Mark/Vin): Can't quit. I need the money for college. I want to take acting classes at Hunter College.

Jed (Irving): Think about majoring in English, Mark. Writing is a good skill if the acting doesn't work out.

Ian (Mark/Vin): Let me think about that. If I can't act in the films, I guess I could write the scripts.

Will (Paul): You are really sure of yourself, aren't you?

Maria (Narrator): Vin is so sure of himself that he moves to Los Angeles before finishing college. He takes a job selling lightbulbs over the phone. He also tries to get acting jobs. But directors don't know what to do with him. Finally he goes back to New York. He talks with his parents.

Jed (Irving): What are you going to do next?

Ian (Mark/Vin): I guess I'll go back to being a bouncer. I want to work on my writing, and hang out with the guys.

Taneka (Delora): I found a book that might be helpful. It's about how to make films for little money. Why don't you take a look at it?

Ian (Mark/Vin): Thanks, Mom. This looks pretty good.

Maria (Narrator): The book is just what Vin needs. He puts together his first film. The film is *Multi-Facial.* He spends only $3,000. He shows the film at Manhattan's Anthology Film Archives. The audience loves it. He is invited to show it at the 1995 Cannes Film Festival in France. Back home, his mom and dad read the papers about the film festival.

Jed (Irving): Look, Delora. The critics liked Mark's film.

Taneka (Delora): What do they say?

Jed (Irving): They say he's an exciting new talent!

Taneka (Delora): New? He's only new to them! If they only knew that he's been at this since he was a little kid!

Jed (Irving): He has worked hard, hasn't he? I wonder what he'll do next.. . .

Maria (Narrator): As everyone knows, Vin Diesel goes on to many film roles. He has a small role in *Saving Private Ryan.* He stars in *The Fast and the Furious* and *A Man Apart.* He becomes successful and famous. And now to close our play, we'll hear some important words from Vin.

Ian (Mark/Vin): It's all about determination and persistence—which is why you should be passionate about what you're doing.. . . So get your team together, and get your confidence together.*

*Quote from *Writers Guild Forum,* 1997.

Cross Outs

Vin Diesel

	A	B	C
1	acting	Mark	be
2	writing	France	determined
3	persistent	Paul	bouncer
4	and	confident	*Multi-Facial*

1. Cross out the 2 names of the Vincent twins in column B.

2. Cross out Vin's job in row 3.

3. Cross out the name of Vin's first film in row 4.

4. Cross out 2 words for what Vin studies in column A.

5. Cross out where the Cannes Film Festival is held in row 2.

Write the remaining words in order below.

_____ _____, _____, _____

_____.

Jean Driscoll

Marathon Athlete

Summary

Jean Driscoll, born with spina bifida on November 18, 1966, could walk with some difficulty until she injured her hip just before her fourteenth birthday. Then she endured a series of excruciating surgeries followed by body casts. Her hope that she'd be able to walk again was dashed when the doctor realized she lacked the muscle development necessary to hold her hip in place. During a year of surgeries, she fell behind in her classes and transferred to a public school. Another student with spina bifida introduced her to wheelchair sports, which engaged her competitive spirit. She continued competing after flunking out of her first semester at college. She was recruited for the athletic program at the University of Illinois, where she was encouraged to train for a marathon. By 2000, Jean set a record for winning eight Boston Marathons.

Presentation Suggestions

The stage can be enhanced with sports equipment, such as soccer balls and basketballs. Consider having Jean, Jim, and Marty Morse read their parts from wheelchairs. The doctor can wear a white coat. Other props include posters from track and race events.

Related Books and Media

- Driscoll, Jean, and Janet and Geoff Benge. *Determined to Win: The Overcoming Spirit of Jean Driscoll.* Colorado Springs, CO: Waterbrook Press, 2000.

- Kaminsky, Marty. *Uncommon Champions: Fifteen Athletes Who Battled Back.* Honesdale, PA: Boyds Mills Press, 2000.

- *Sports, Everyone!: Recreation and Sports for the Physically Challenged of All Ages.* Cleveland, OH: Conway Greene, 1995.

- Jean Driscoll: www.jeandriscoll.com

Characters

Narrator 1	Dad
Narrator 2	Doctor
Marcia, *Jean's friend*	Jim, *Jean's classmate*
Jean Driscoll	Brad Hedrick, *Athletic Supervisor at the University of Illinois*
Mom	Marty Morse, *University of Illinois coach*
Francie, *Jean's sister*	Announcer

Jean Driscoll
Marathon Athlete

Scene 1

Narrator 1: Jean, age ten, has spina bifida. This condition affects the spinal cord and its protective coverings. It is hard for her to walk. She also looks odd when she walks.

Narrator 2: Jean just wants to be like the other kids. She also knows how to work hard at something she wants. One day she is playing with her friend, Marcia. Marcia lives nearby.

Marcia: Look, Jean. I don't need my training wheels anymore!

Jean: I wish I could ride without training wheels.

Marcia: I wish you could too. Watch me, Jean! It's fun!

Narrator 1: Jean notices Marcia's little brother's bike.

Jean: I bet I could ride that bike!

Narrator 2: Jean climbs on Ricky's small bike. Her feet touch the ground. She pushes off. She doesn't know how to balance well. But she keeps trying. She tries all day. Finally she gets it. Then she goes home for supper.

Jean: Mom, I learned how to ride without training wheels!

Mom: What? How can that be?

Jean: I'll show you.

Narrator 1: Jean takes her mother outside. She gets on Ricky's bike and rides it.

Mom: Jean, that's great! Dad can take the training wheels off your bike later.

Narrator 2: Jean loves riding her bike. When she is twelve, she bikes with her twin brothers 13 miles to her aunt's house. Her bike is a one-speed. That makes going up hills very hard. Her legs just aren't strong enough.

Narrator 1: Jean wants a ten-speed bike. Her family doesn't have much money because of her doctor bills. When she is thirteen, however, her school has a read-a-thon. The person who reads the most books will win a ten-speed bike. Jean discusses the contest with her older sister, Francie.

Jean: I'm going win the read-a-thon so I can get a new bike.

Francie: How are you going to do that?

Jean: I've been going to lots of people's houses. Most say they'll sponsor me.

Francie: But you don't read very fast.

Jean: Well, I'm going to read lots of books. I have to win this contest.

Narrator 2: Jean reads many books. She collects the money from her sponsors. She turns it in to her teacher.

Narrator 1: Finally the contest is over. Jean wins the bike! Her hard work has paid off.

Scene 2

Narrator 2: Jean is almost fourteen. She enjoys high school. She can't play in sports so she works hard at learning. One day she gets on her bike after babysitting. She turns too far when going into the street.

Narrator 1: Jean's bike tips over. She falls down on her left hip. She lies there for a moment. She can hardly move because of the pain.

Jean: *(to herself)* I have to get up. I have to get home. I can do this. I can do this.

Narrator 2: Jean starts to feel a little better. She gets up and carefully rides home. She feels okay for a while. Then she finds her legs aren't working right. Her dad sees her trying to stand up.

Dad: What's wrong, Jean?

Jean: Something's wrong with my leg. I can't stand up.

Dad: Let me take a look at you.

Narrator 1: Jean uses crutches for a few days. Then she gets some x-rays. Her mother talks with the doctor.

Doctor: Jean has injured her hip. She'll need several surgeries. First we have to get her hip back in the right place. Then we'll start on the surgeries.

Mom: How long will it take?

Doctor: I don't know. It depends on how fast she heals. She'll need to wear a body cast between the surgeries.

Narrator 2: Soon Jean is at the hospital for traction. This process will get her hip moved into the right place. A lot of kids with spina bifida have no feeling in their legs. Jean does. However, the doctor doesn't give her any pain medicine.

Narrator 1: The doctor uses several needles on her hip. Jean screams when he starts drilling on her hip. A triangle sticks out of both sides of Jean's thigh. This is attached to the traction equipment.

Narrator 2: For ten days, Jean lies in bed. Then she has her first surgery. After the surgery she has a body cast. It starts above her waist and goes down to her left foot and her right knee. She stays in the hospital for four weeks.

Scene 3

Narrator 1: Jean endures nearly a year of surgeries and being in a body cast. Finally the cast is cut off. The doctor brings in her latest x-rays.

Doctor: I'm very sorry to bring you this news. Your hip won't stay in the right place. We can't do anything else. You have to get used to things the way they are.

Jean: Will I be able to walk?

Doctor: If you work hard, you'll be able to walk a little. When you go to school you'll have to use a wheelchair.

Jean: But what about the surgeries? I went through five surgeries. I'm worse off than before.

Doctor: I'm sorry, Jean.

Narrator 2: Jean is upset at first. But soon she starts working on walking. She finally goes back to school. She has to use a wheelchair. For more than a year, she has had a tutor. Jean realizes she's fallen behind. She struggles to catch up.

Narrator 1: That spring she gets her report card. It's all D's and F's. Jean asks her parents if she can transfer from the parochial school to a public school. She thinks it will be easier to get through high school.

Narrator 2: That fall she starts at Custer High School. She uses a wheelchair to get around. She meets Jim, who is also in a wheelchair.

Jim: Hey. How are you?

Jean: Fine.

Jim: Do you play wheelchair soccer? Would you like to come with me Saturday?

Jean: You can't play soccer without legs.

Jim: Sure you can. We play from our wheelchairs.

Jean: No, thanks. I have something to do.

Narrator 1: Jim doesn't take no for an answer. He keeps asking Jean to play. Finally she agrees. She finds she loves wheelchair soccer. She decides to try every sport she can. She loves ice hockey and water skiing. Before long, Jean graduates from high school. She also buys a car with hand controls. Then she leaves for the University of Wisconsin.

Scene 4

Narrator 2: College proves to be a tough time for Jean. Her parents get a divorce. She has more health problems. She flunks out after one semester.

Narrator 1: Jean gets a job as a nanny. She also continues her wheelchair sports. Dr. Brad Hedrick sees her play a game of soccer. He runs the athletics program for disabled students at the University of Illinois.

Brad Hedrick: You played a great game, Jean.

Jean: Thanks.

Brad Hedrick: How about coming to play on our wheelchair basketball team? I could use you.

Jean: I don't know . . .

Brad Hedrick: We have great coaches. You'd get to travel for the games. You'd love it.

Jean: Let me think about it.

Brad Hedrick: I'll send you some information.

Narrator 2: Jean decides she wants to be in the program. First she has to prove that she can pass a semester of college classes. She works hard and is accepted to the University of Illinois.

Narrator 1: Before long Jean is competing in track events. She gets a sponsor who makes sure she has a good racing wheelchair. She starts winning the sprinting events. She even wins events in London, England. She works hard at her studies so she won't flunk out again. Her coach is happy with her work. But he pushes her even more.

Marty Morse: Jean, you do great in your events. But you should try a marathon.

Jean: I don't want to race for even 1500 meters. I could never do a marathon.

Marty Morse: It would be good training for you.

Jean: But you said yourself that I'm doing fine.

Marty Morse: That's true. But don't you want to do well at the Paralympics?

Jean: You know that I do.

Marty Morse: The distance training would help you compete better.

Jean: I'll think about it.

Narrator 2: Jean thinks that people who race more than 26 miles must be crazy. Then she has to train for the Olympics in Barcelona, Spain. She decides that the distance training might help. She agrees to race in the Chicago Marathon.

Scene 5

Narrator 1: Jean trains hard. She surprises herself. She finishes the marathon in just under two hours. Marty Morse meets her at the finish line.

Marty Morse: Congratulations, Jean!

Jean: Thanks!

Marty Morse: Now you can do the Boston Marathon! You've qualified for it!

Jean: I don't want to do another one, Marty. This was just for training.

Marty Morse: But this is a big deal, Jean! How can you *not* do the Boston Marathon?

Jean: I don't know, Marty . . .

Narrator 2: Marty works on Jean. Finally she tells him she'll do one—just one. She practices harder than ever. Finally the day of the race arrives. She knows she has to beat Connie Hansen. Jean does better going up the hills. Connie does better coming down the hills.

Narrator 1: When Jean hits mile 23, she realizes she's winning the race. She keeps working hard. She is amazed to hear the announcer's voice.

Announcer: Jean Driscoll from Illinois comes in at 1 hour, 43 minutes, and 17 seconds. She beats the world record by almost seven minutes!

Narrator 2: Jean's life changes at that moment. She wins a lot of money. She also gets a lot of attention from television and newspapers. She goes back to school. But she knows she'll keep training for more marathons.

Narrator 1: Jean goes on to graduate from college in 1991 at age 24. She wins her eighth Boston Marathon in 2000. Jean is no longer that little girl who wished she could be like everyone else. She has proven she is a winner.

Cross Outs

Jean Driscoll

	A	B	C
1	soccer	Jean	ice hockey
2	runs	crutches	wheelchair
3	on	wheels	to
4	basketball	spina bifida	win

1. Cross out the name of Jean's condition in column B.

2. Cross out 2 of the sports Jean plays in high school in row 1.

3. Cross out the sport Jean plays in college in column A.

4. Cross out the 2 words in row 2 for things that help Jean get around.

Write the remaining words in order below.

_____ _____ _____ _____

_____ _____.

David Eckstein

Baseball Player

Summary

When the Anaheim Angels won the 2002 World Series, it really was a case of David slaying Goliath—a bunch of Goliaths, in fact. Angels' shortstop David Eckstein was a key factor in his team's championship. In the American League playoffs, he helped the Angels beat the New York Yankees. In the World Series, he helped beat the San Francisco Giants, led by their all-star out-fielder, Barry Bonds. That's quite a feat for a player who stands only 5' 7" and weighs 175 pounds. All his life, Eckstein was told that he was too small to play in the big leagues. But in Oc-tober 2002, he proved his critics wrong. And he did it with his heart and his head as much as he did with his glove or his bat.

Presentation Suggestions

Before, during, or after reading the play, students can watch highlights of the 2002 World Series to see how Eckstein helped his club win. Students can also research newspapers and mag-azine articles about Eckstein to find out how valuable his teammates say he is to the team.

Related Book and Media

- *Anaheim Angels: World Series Champions*, by Associated Press, Sports Publishing LLC. Sports Publishing, Inc., 2002.
- Official Site of the Anaheim Angels: www.angelsbaseball.com

Characters

Narrator 1

Narrator 2

University of Florida baseball coach

David Eckstein

Lou Wrenn, *a baseball scout*

Whitey Eckstein, *David's father*

Darrin Erstad, *member of the Anaheim Angels*

Garrett Anderson, *member of the Anaheim Angels*

Security Guard

Mike Scioscia, *manager of the Anaheim Angels*

Adam Kennedy, *Angels infielder*

San Francisco Giants' pitcher

David Perno, *manager of the University of Georgia baseball team*

Baseball player

Tim Salmon, *member of the Anaheim Angels*

David Eckstein
Baseball Player

Scene 1

Narrator 1: It is two months before the start of the baseball season. The coach for the University of Florida baseball team sits in his office. He is talking on the phone to his wife.

Florida Baseball Coach: Yes, honey. I should be home early today. The real work won't start for another four or five weeks yet. We already have—

Narrator 2: The coach hears a sound coming from the indoor batting cages: *Thwack! Thwack! Thwack!*

Narrator 1: The coach pauses for a moment before he speaks again.

Florida Baseball Coach: We have most of our team set. But in four or five weeks, about seventy kids will show up and try to get a place on the team. Yes, that's right. The "walk-ons."

Narrator 2: The coach is interrupted again: *Thwack! Thwack! Thwack!*

Florida Baseball Coach: Honey, I'll have to call you back.

Narrator 1: The coach heads toward the batting cage. In it, a machine tosses fastballs to a young man. His name is David Eckstein. He hits pitch after pitch after pitch.

Florida Baseball Coach: Excuse me.

Narrator 2: David switches the machine off.

David Eckstein: Yes, sir?

Florida Baseball Coach: Are you a student here?

David Eckstein: Yes sir. I'm a freshman.

Florida Baseball Coach: A freshman? At the high school, or here at the university?

David Eckstein: Here, sir. I want to try out for the team as a walk-on.

Florida Baseball Coach: I'm not looking at walk-ons for at least a month.

David Eckstein: I know, sir. But one of the coaches said I could use the cage. I wanted to get some practice in. If you want, though, I'll clear out.

Florida Baseball Coach: Uh . . . no. Go ahead, uh . . .

David Eckstein: Eckstein, sir. David Eckstein.

Florida Baseball Coach: All right. You keep practicing, Eckstein. And if you don't make it as a walk-on . . . well, hang around anyway. We may need a spare body to help out in practices.

David Eckstein: *(smiling)* Yes sir. Thanks very much.

Narrator 1: The coach turns to leave. David switches the pitching machine back on. *Thwack! Thwack! Thwack!*

Scene 2

Narrator 2: David makes the team as a second baseman. He helps lead them to the College World Series. Still, very few major league scouts notice him.

Narrator 1: One scout who does notice him is Lou Wrenn. He works for the Boston Red Sox. One day, Wrenn visits David's father.

Lou Wrenn: Mr. Eckstein, I think David has a good future in pro baseball. I think that he can make a living in the game.

Whitey Eckstein: That's great.

Lou Wrenn: Yeah. He might play for three or four years in the minor leagues. After that, he could become a minor league coach. Maybe even a manager.

Whitey Eckstein: That's it, huh? A career in the minors?

Lou Wrenn: I'm afraid that David just doesn't have the physical tools to play on the big-league level. Still he has enough brains and heart to make a good living in the game.

Whitey Eckstein: *(smiling)* Well I think he's going to do more than that. You see, my boy is tougher than you know.

Lou Wrenn: Really?

Whitey Eckstein: Several years ago, two of David's sisters and his brother all had to have kidney transplants. They got through it with flying colors. Still, I've always known that David is the toughest of us all. He won't quit. He just needs a chance. He'll make the most of it.

Lou Wrenn: Great. I'm offering him a contract in the Red Sox minor league. Let's see what he can do.

Scene 3

Narrator 2: David plays for the Red Sox's minor league team. Then he has a long batting slump. They release him in 1999. Soon he is signed by the Anaheim Angels. They see something special in the way he plays.

Narrator 1: In 2001, the Angels' regular second baseman breaks his finger in spring training. David fills in for him. He wins a position on the major league team for the season.

Narrator 2: During the 2001–2002 off-season, several Anaheim Angels visit a shopping mall. They are there for an autograph session. Eckstein is among them.

Darrin Erstad: Man, look at that line!

Tim Salmon: Yeah, there's a real buzz in the air. The fans like our chances this year.

Garrett Anderson: I do, too. If our pitching stays healthy, I think we've got a shot.

David Eckstein: We definitely have a shot. I think we can win it all.

Darrin Erstad: *(to Eckstein)* Hey! Are you still hanging around here? *(to a nearby security guard)* Officer? Officer! This kid keeps sneaking up and sitting at our table.

Narrator 1: The rest of the Angels snicker to themselves.

David Eckstein: *(grinning and shaking his head)* Not again . . .

Security Guard: All right, kid. Let's go. You can't sit with the ballplayers.

David Eckstein: Officer, I *am* one of the ballplayers.

Security Guard: Right. And I'm Michael Jordan. Look, you can't be more than fifteen years old. I'm calling your parents and telling them to come and get you.

Narrator 2: The other players burst out laughing.

Tim Salmon: No, officer, we're just kidding around. He really is on the team.

Narrator 1: The officer looks at Eckstein.

Security Guard: Just how old *are* you?

David Eckstein: I'm 27.

Security Guard: *(shaking his head)* All right. If you say so.

Narrator 2: The other players keep laughing as the guard walks away.

David Eckstein: *(grinning)* Very funny, guys. Very funny.

Darrin Erstad: *(laughing)* You really should grow a beard or something.

David Eckstein: I did. But my parents didn't like it, so I shaved it off.

Narrator 1: The players laugh again.

Scene 4

Narrator 2: By the end of the 2002 season, no one is laughing anymore. The Angels make it to the post-season. First, they beat the heavily favored New York Yankees. Then they defeat the Minnesota Twins. Finally, they face the San Francisco Giants in the World Series.

Narrator 1: Eckstein is now the club's starting shortstop. He is in the thick of each post-season scoring drive. He sparks rally after rally. He helps lead the team to the world championship.

Narrator 2: In the Angels' locker room, much of the praise is directed at Eckstein. The fans call him "the Ecks Factor."

Mike Scioscia: He's the sparkplug for our club. He plays at a level that might surprise some people. But we understand his heart and his head. We know how talented he really is.

Adam Kennedy: If you want to see how valuable David is, talk to our big hitters. They drive in a lot of runs because he's on base all the time. He knows the game. He makes all the plays.

Narrator 1: In the Giants' locker room, players are amazed by the tiny ballplayer.

Giants' Pitcher: He's just a pain. He'll take a pitch in the arm or the ribs just to get on base. Then he'll scamper around and drive you nuts. He plays the game the way it's supposed to be played.

Narrator 2: As the celebration continues, Eckstein is asked about his own talent.

David Eckstein: I'm the same player I was when I was a kid. Even in Little League, I was the guy trying to get on base for the big hitters. The guy who had to play good defense and not make many mistakes. I'm far from a perfect player. I mean, I have confidence, but I need to get much better.

Scene 5

Narrator 1: It is winter, 2003. David's brother is a coach with the University of Georgia baseball team. David is working out with the team. None of the college players realize who he is. Many simply think he is a freshman walk-on.

Narrator 2: At the end of the practice, Eckstein sprints off the field. Many of the Georgia players take their time and jog off the field. Manager David Perno notices.

David Perno: Hey, guys. Guys! Come here. I want you to meet someone. *(pointing at Eckstein)* This is David Eckstein of the Anaheim Angels.

Narrator 1: The players are amazed.

David Perno: If a world-champion ballplayer can run on and off the field, we can too, can't we?

Narrator 2: The players say nothing.

David Perno: I want to see you guys running on and off this field for, let's say . . . the next half hour. Let's go!

Narrator 1: The team takes off. One of the players lags behind.

Baseball Player: Umm . . . Mr. Eckstein? When you're done, can you give me a few pointers on bunting?

David Eckstein: *(smiling)* Sure. I'd be happy to.

Baseball Player: Great! Thanks!

Narrator 2: The player takes off and follows his teammates.

Cross Outs

David Eckstein

	A	B	C
1	Red Sox	coach	majors
2	short	scout	Angel
3	Yankees	beats	minors
4	shortstop	Giants	pitcher

1. Cross out 2 kinds of teams in column C.

2. Cross out the names of 2 teams in column A.

3. Cross out 2 kinds of playing positions in row 4.

4. Cross out 2 names for jobs in baseball in column B.

Write the remaining words in order below.

_____ _____ _____ _____ .

Michael J. Fox

Actor

Summary

Michael J. Fox started acting when he was in elementary school. He dropped out of high school and left Canada for Hollywood. He got a few roles right away, but he wasn't successful until his role as Alex Keaton in *Family Ties*. When Fox was only thirty, he was diagnosed with Parkinson's disease. By this time he had married actress Tracy Pollan. Fox realized he needed to stop drinking and get help from a therapist. He also finally completed high school by taking the G.E.D. exam. Fox now works to raise money for Parkinson's disease research.

Presentation Suggestions

Jamie Brant can be either a male or a female. Brant and Fox can sit at a table or on stools as if they are having an interview. The other characters can stand in the background until they read their roles. Students can be dressed in regular clothes.

Related Book and Media

- Fox, Michael J. *Lucky Man.* New York: Hyperion, 2002.

- Information about Fox, his work with Parkinson's disease: http://www.michaeljfox.org

Characters

Narrator 1	Ross Jones, *acting teacher*
Narrator 2	Phyllis Fox, *Michael's mother*
Jamie Brant, *high school reporter*	Judy Wiener, *casting director of* Family Ties
Michael J. Fox, *actor*	Tracy Pollan, *actor and Michael's wife*

 **Michael J. Fox**
Actor

Scene 1

Narrator 1: Jamie Brant is a reporter for a high school newspaper. Jamie is meeting with Michael J. Fox. Fox has agreed to an interview.

Jamie Brant: Good morning, Mr. Fox. Thank you for agreeing to talk with me.

Michael J. Fox: You're welcome. Let's get started.

Jamie Brant: Can you tell me about what you were like in school? Were you a good student?

Michael J. Fox: I was good in some subjects. I loved to draw, write long poems and stories, and play the guitar. But don't ask me about classes like math. I was bad in those!

Jamie Brant: How did you get started in acting?

Michael J. Fox: I was in a few school plays when I was a kid. I loved the attention. Then I got into high school. I liked losing myself in a role.

Jamie Brant: What was your first big break?

Narrator 2: Fox thinks for a minute. Then he begins to talk about what it was like to be in high school in Canada in 1977. Brant can actually see Fox's acting teacher talking to Fox.

Ross Jones: Hey, Mike. Take a look at this! The CBC* is starting a new TV show. They are looking for a bright twelve-year-old kid.

Michael J. Fox: I could play a kid. This might be the first time I'm be glad to be short!

Ross Jones: You're sure bright enough!

Michael J. Fox: Do you think they'd see me?

Ross Jones: I already talked to them. They'll see you. Get your mom to take you to their studios.

Narrator 1: Fox's mom takes him to the tryouts. There are lots of kids waiting their turns.

Phyllis Fox: Do you want to go through the lines?

Michael J. Fox: No, I'm okay.

Narrator 2: Michael is asked lots of questions. He gets called back to read again. Then he gets the part. Michael J. Fox is on his way. But he has a long way to go.

Scene 2

Narrator 1: Jamie Brant checks the tape recorder. Then Jamie asks the next question.

Jamie Brant: Did you make a lot of money?

Michael J. Fox: *(laughing)* I made $600 every week that summer. I made almost $6,000. Let me tell you, that was a lot of money for a kid!

Jamie Brant: What was it like to go back to school?

Michael J. Fox: I went into eleventh grade that fall. I didn't see much point of high school then. I had gotten used to making money.

Jamie Brant: Did you get more acting jobs?

Michael J. Fox: Yes. But I wasn't doing very well. My parents let me drop out of school so I could act full time.

Narrator 2: Once again, Brant can see Fox's life as if it were happening. Michael is talking with his parents.

Michael J. Fox: *(to his parents)* Mom and Dad, I want to go to Hollywood.

Bill Fox: Are you sure?

Michael J. Fox: Yes.

Phyllis Fox: You have a good start going here, son. You're making good money.

Michael J. Fox: I know. But I know I can get work in Hollywood. I look young and they need young actors.

Phyllis Fox: You're not even eighteen yet.

Michael J. Fox: That's why I need you to agree to this.

Bill Fox: Well, if that's what you want to do, I think you'll get it done. I'll take you there.

Narrator 1: Bill Fox drives Michael to California. A few days later, Mike calls his mother.

Michael J. Fox: Mom, guess what!

Phyllis Fox: You sound excited. You must have good news!

Michael J. Fox: I'm coming home!

Phyllis Fox: I don't understand. Is that good?

Michael J. Fox: I'm going to be in a movie! And I have an agent!

Phyllis Fox: That's wonderful, Michael. What's the movie?

Michael J. Fox: It's called *Midnight Madness*. It's a Disney movie. Dad and I are going to come home so I can pack. We'll see you soon.

Narrator 2: Michael J. Fox turns eighteen years old on June 9, 1979. The next day he flies to Los Angeles and begins his Hollywood career.

Scene 3

Narrator 1: Jamie Brant starts asking Fox more questions.

Jamie Brant: You must have thought you had it made! Your first movie!

Michael J. Fox: I was pretty excited. But the movie wasn't even close to a hit.

Jamie Brant: What about TV?

Michael J. Fox: I got a few roles in TV shows. And I did some commercials. But I was almost starving.

Jamie Brant: But weren't you getting paid?

Michael J. Fox: Yes, but I was young and not very smart. I had some managers who took advantage of me. I was never good at math. I didn't keep a budget. I just didn't pay attention to business.

Jamie Brant: What changed?

Michael J. Fox: I started paying attention to my money. But I wasn't getting much work then. Finally, in 1982, things turned around. I had read for a part in a TV show called *Family Ties*. But I didn't get it at first. Let me tell you about it.

Narrator 2: Once again, Jamie can see everything as if it were happening right there. Jamie can see Michael answer the phone.

Michael J. Fox: Hello.

Judy Wiener: Michael, this is Judy Wiener. We want you to read for *Family Ties* again.

Michael J. Fox: No problem.

Judy Wiener: You'll be reading for the writers. Gary Goldberg, the producer and creator, will be there this time.

Michael J. Fox: Do you have any suggestions?

Judy Wiener: Just one. Try to make the guy a little more lovable.

Michael J. Fox: Sure.

Narrator 1: Michael does a great job. He is very funny. Gary Goldberg laughs a lot. Fox gets the role of Alex Keaton in *Family Ties*. The show becomes a big hit. His future is bright.

Scene 4

Narrator 2: Jamie Brant and Fox talk about his great success in *Family Ties*. Fox does roles in movies when he can. One movie, *Back to the Future*, is a huge hit. But life isn't exactly great for Fox.

Jamie Brant: What was it like to be a huge star? Did you enjoy making big money?

Michael J. Fox: I wanted to act. I didn't spend a lot of time worrying about the money. I did spend a lot of time drinking. And that was a mistake. Many times I had to go to work after spending the night out drinking.

Jamie Brant: Didn't anyone say anything?

Michael J. Fox: No one did until Tracy Pollan came along. She played my girlfriend on *Family Ties* for a while in 1985 and 1986. She was the first person to tell me that drinking might be a problem.

Jamie Brant: You married Tracy, right?

Michael J. Fox: Not right away. She had a boyfriend when she was on *Family Ties*. We met again in 1987. This time she didn't have a boyfriend. We were just like the people we played on *Family Ties*. We fell in love. We got married in 1988. Then my life changed. This was not a good change.

Narrator 1: Jamie sits back and imagines Michael's new challenge.

Michael J. Fox: *(talking to himself)* It's nothing to worry about. It's just my little finger twitching. I just need to get more rest, stop drinking. It will be fine.

Narrator 2: Fox decides to call Tracy.

Michael J. Fox: Hi Tracy.

Tracy Pollan: How is the movie going?

Michael J. Fox: It's going well, but I had a little trouble this morning.

Tracy Pollan: Tell me about it. Are you okay?

Michael J. Fox: I'm fine. Well, I think I'm fine.

Narrator 1: Michael tells her how his finger has been shaking all morning.

Tracy Pollan: It's probably nothing. But maybe you should talk to a doctor about it.

Michael J. Fox: Well, I'll see how I feel. I'll talk with you later.

Narrator 2: Fox goes to a doctor. The doctor thinks Fox had a minor injury to his funny bone. For the next few months, Mike goes back to work. He begins to have more symptoms. A year later he and Tracy are on vacation. Fox decides to go for a run. As he gets near the house, Tracy meets him.

Tracy Pollan: Are you okay? The left side of your body doesn't look right. Your arm isn't swinging. I think you should see a doctor.

Michael J. Fox: OK. I'll go when we get back to the city.

Narrator 1: Michael sees a doctor in New York City. After some tests, the doctor tells him to see a neurologist. This doctor gives him the news that changes his life. He tells Fox that he has Parkinson's disease.

Narrator 2: For a while Fox refuses to believe the doctor. He is just thirty years old. After all, Parkinson's is for *old* people. He tells Tracy the news.

Michael J. Fox: The doctor said I have Parkinson's disease.

Tracy Pollan: How can that be? You're too young!

Michael J. Fox: I know. I know. Maybe it's all a big mistake.

Tracy Pollan: You need to see another doctor. We need to be sure.

Michael J. Fox: I will, Tracy. We've just started our family. I just can't believe this has happened.

Scene 5

Narrator 1: Jamie starts the interview again.

Jamie Brant: This was really bad news. How did you handle it?

Michael J. Fox: I was so angry at first. I just couldn't accept it. I wondered what could have caused it. Was I exposed to some chemical? Did I drink too much? I'd had some concussions playing hockey. Maybe those caused it.

Jamie Brant: Could the doctors figure out the cause?

Michael J. Fox: No. There was just no real way to know. We always want to know the answers. Sometimes there aren't any.

Jamie Brant: What about drugs? Did anything help?

Michael J. Fox: I started taking some drugs that helped. I did something else too. I quit drinking. It was hard work. But I haven't had a drink for more than ten years.

Jamie Brant: What about your work?

Michael J. Fox: I kept working. I felt like I had to, even though I really didn't need the money. But it got harder and I realized I needed more help.

Jamie Brant: What kind of help?

Michael J. Fox: I went to see a therapist. Talking about my problems helped. It took a lot of time and it was hard work. By 1994 I felt a lot better. In fact, I did something I should have done a long time ago.

Jamie Brant: What was that?

Michael J. Fox: I took the G.E.D. exam. I finally graduated from high school! Then life got even better. We had twin girls the next spring.

Jamie Brant: When did you decide to go public about Parkinson's disease?

Michael J. Fox: There had been some rumors. And I was tired of working so hard to hide the problems. I decided to tell my story in 1998. I realized that money was needed for research. So that's my new job. Speaking out.

Jamie Brant: I have one last question. Does being a celebrity help?

Michael J. Fox: You bet it does! I've met other people with Parkinson's disease. They tell me they don't care if I get more attention. They just tell me that if I get to speak into a microphone to start talking. And that's exactly what I do!

* The CBC is the Canadian Broadcasting Corporation.

 **Cross Outs**

Michael J. Fox

	A	**B**	**C**
1	G.E.D.	Parkinson's	Fox
2	*Back to the Future*	acts	*Midnight Madness*
3	*Family Ties*	up	and
4	speaks	out	Canada

1. Cross out Fox's country of birth in column C.

2. Cross out the name of Fox's first movie in row 2.

3. Cross out the name of the show where Fox met Tracy Pollan in row A.

4. Cross out the name of Fox's hit movie in row 2.

5. Cross out the name of Fox's disease in row 1.

6. Cross out the name of the exam Fox took in column A.

Write the remaining words in order below.

_____ _____ _____ _____

_____ _____.

Zina Garrison

Tennis Champion

Summary

Zina Garrison began playing tennis as a young girl. A natural athlete who loved to compete, Zina faced prejudice as one of few black tennis players. Born in 1963, she turned pro in 1982. Her highest singles ranking was number 4, and she earned more than $4,000,000 during her career. However, Zina harbored a secret. Wanting to look like the slim white women she competed against, Zina turned to bulimia to control her weight. As her health, career, and marriage failed, she realized she had to win back her health.

Presentation Suggestions

The setting can be informal, with a few props to indicate a home environment. Scene 4 could be a school, club, or outdoor setting. Characters can be dressed in regular clothes or tennis clothes, as appropriate.

Related Books and Media

- Garrison, Zina, and Doug Smith. *Zina: My Life in Women's Tennis.* Berkeley, CA: Frog, 2001.

- Kaminsky, Marty. *Uncommon Champions: Fifteen Athletes Who Battled Back.* Honesdale, PA: Boyds Mills Press, 2000.

- Zina Garrison: www.zinagarrison.org

Characters

Narrator 1

Narrator 2

Mama

Zina Garrison

Rodney Garrison, *Zina's brother*

John, *Zina's coach*

Lori McNeil, *tennis player*

Chandra, *student*

Tanesha, *student*

Bryce, *student*

Dewayne, *student*

Kaleena, *student*

Zina Garrison
Tennis Champion

Scene 1

Narrator 1: The time is the late 1960s. Zina lives with her mom, brother, and four sisters. Zina's father died just after she was born in 1963.

Narrator 2: Zina's family lives near downtown Houston. Their house is small with a big yard. Lots of kids hang out there.

Narrator 1: Mama works as a nurses' aide. But she has diabetes, so she is sick a lot. Zina has to help out around the house.

Mama: Zina, they're giving away food down at the church. Go get in line.

Zina Garrison: Mama, you know I hate to do that. Can't you go?

Mama: Girl, I've already gone. They won't give me more. You go and get some cheese. Go on now.

Zina Garrison: *(reluctantly)* All right, Mama.

Mama: And when you get back, Rodney will be starting his barbeque.

Zina Garrison: Barbeque! Great! See you later, Mama.

Narrator 2: Rodney is Zina's older brother. He plays baseball at college. Later Zina plays catch with him.

Rodney Garrison: Zina, how did your field day at school go?

Zina Garrison: You know I won all the sprints.

Rodney Garrison: Running short races isn't everything. You need to do the long ones too.

Zina Garrison: Those are boring. I like the short races. You run. You're done.

Rodney Garrison: You are good. That's true. You should try tennis.

Zina Garrison: What do you know about tennis?

Rodney Garrison: Carol plays tennis.

Zina Garrison: Carol? Your girlfriend? *(chanting)* Rodney and Carol sitting in a tree . . .

Rodney Garrison: You stop that! I'm serious. This guy at the park teaches tennis. You should go try it.

Zina Garrison: Maybe . . .

Narrator 1: A few weeks later Zina watches John hit balls to another player.

Zina Garrison: *(to herself)* That looks easy.

Narrator 2: A ball rolls over to Zina.

John: What are you doing? *(pausing)* Do you want to play tennis?

Zina Garrison: It looks pretty easy. Maybe.

John: Well, let's see what you can do.

Narrator 2: Zina tries it. She learns quickly.

John: You know, you could be pretty good. Why don't you come to my lessons?

Zina Garrison: I have to think about it. It is kind of fun.

Scene 2

Narrator 1: John starts teaching Zina. For a while, she prefers riding her bike. But before long she falls in love with the game. She starts playing doubles with Lori McNeil. They are both ten years old. They are also both black players. Few black people play tennis. Even fewer black people compete.

Narrator 2: Playing tennis becomes Zina's life. She and Lori find out that white people don't like them playing tennis much.

Zina Garrison: Lori, I am so sick of the attitude of those officials.

Lori McNeil: What do you mean?

Zina Garrison: That guy asked for my birth certificate.

Lori McNeil: They always think you're older than you are.

Zina Garrison: I'm not *that* big! They just hate to see their white girls get beat.

Lori McNeil: John sets the officials straight. He tells them all the other kids should have to prove their ages.

Zina Garrison: That shut them up.

Lori McNeil: Yeah. But it won't last. They really don't like us, do they?

Zina Garrison: No. That just makes me want to show them up more. They don't like it when we win.

Lori McNeil: I guess we'll just have to win more!

Narrator 1: Zina and Lori keep winning. Zina plays in her first American Tennis Association Nationals in 1975. The ATA black kids come from all over the United States to play tennis.

Narrator 2: She sprains her ankle, preventing her win. However, in 1977, she does win. Zina is on her way to success.

Scene 3

Narrator 1: Zina has to prove herself in school too. John won't let her compete if her grades aren't good. Mama decides to send her to a mostly white school for junior high. Zina doesn't like it.

Zina Garrison: Mama, why do you make me go to that school?

Mama: What's wrong with it?

Zina Garrison: There aren't many black kids there.

Mama: So? You can get along with anyone. That's what I've taught you.

Zina Garrison: How? They don't mix. The white kids don't eat with us black kids. Everyone stays with their own kind.

Mama: They have good teachers.

Zina Garrison: Those teachers aren't so good.

Mama: What do you mean?

Zina Garrison: They pick on us black kids.

Mama: Are you sure?

Zina Garrison: Mama, I know they do. If one of us gets a good grade they say we must have cheated.

Narrator 2: Finally Mama gives in. She lets Zina go to an all-black high school.

Narrator 1: Zina is happier there. But she doesn't always get good grades. Once she even flunks English.

Mama: Zina, what about this English grade?

Zina Garrison: I'm sorry, Mama.

Mama: You're going to be even sorrier this summer. You have to go to summer school.

Zina Garrison: Mama! Then I can't compete!

Mama: That's right. You know the rules. John agrees.

Zina Garrison: How long do I have to stay out?

Mama: At least a month. That's how long summer school lasts. We'll see after that.

Narrator 2: Zina gets through summer school. She wins more and more at tennis. Her senior year is great. She wins Wimbledon, the U.S. Open, and other titles.

Narrator 1: She wants to be a pro. Then she can earn more money. She talks about it with Lori.

Zina Garrison: Do you want to go pro, Lori?

Lori McNeil: I don't think I'm ready.

Zina Garrison: Are you nuts? Of course you're ready. We could go on tour together.

Lori McNeil: I want to go to college. I can play tennis at college. Then I can turn pro.

Zina Garrison: My mama wants me to go to college too. She's really putting the pressure on.

Lori McNeil: Well, why don't you?

Zina Garrison: I just want to play tennis. You know that.

Narrator 2: Zina's mom finally agrees to let Zina turn pro. It's 1982. Zina's playing gets better and better. Sadly, Mama's health gets worse. Zina tries to get her to take care of herself.

Narrator 1: But her mama loves to eat the wrong foods. She can't change her old habits. It all catches up to her. Before long, she dies. Zina is left only with memories of her mama's love and support.

Scene 4

Narrator 2: Years have passed. It is now the late 1990s. Zina has had a great career in tennis. She has beaten many famous tennis players. She opens doors for other black players. Two of them, Venus and Serena Williams, begin building great tennis careers.

Narrator 1: Zina has a bigger goal now. She wants to help young people play tennis. She also wants to tell them about her secret. Zina talks with some teens.

Zina Garrison: We've talked a lot about my tennis playing. It's time to talk about something else. Do any of you ever feel fat?

Chandra: Fat? Us? What do you mean?

Zina Garrison: You know. You're walking along with some white kids. Any of them have big butts?

Tanesha: Are you kidding? Not them.

Zina Garrison: Right. Almost all are thin—just about perfect. Funny thing about that. When I was your age I looked pretty good. But I thought I had a big butt. I had to wear those tiny skirts made for white women. I wanted to look just like them. Well, that's what I thought. So I took action.

Bryce: What did you do?

Zina Garrison: It was simple. I loved to eat. Especially junk food. I'd eat and eat. But I still wanted to look like the thin girls. So I'd throw up.

Bryce: I've heard of that. It's called bulimia.

Dewayne: Isn't that a girl thing?

Zina Garrison: I thought so at first. Then I found out that a lot of guys have bulimia.

Kaleena: I don't get it. How could you just throw up?

Zina Garrison: It was pretty simple. First, I'd stick my fingers down my throat. That would make me barf. Then it got easier. I'd think about feeling bad. And I'd just barf.

Tanesha: Didn't you feel bad then?

Zina Garrison: Yes. But I didn't want to be fat. That felt worse. And I wanted control of my body. I didn't want to control what I ate. But I could control my weight by purging—throwing up. But the price was high.

Kaleena: What do you mean? Didn't you get skinny?

Zina Garrison: Yes. But bulimia causes lots of problems. My hair got thin. I got blotches on my skin. My nails got soft. My teeth got bad. It even affected my heart rate.

Tanesha: I don't get it. Why? You had everything going for you.

Zina Garrison: Yes. It seemed so. But I was a young black player. There weren't very many like me. But there were a lot of skinny white gals.

Dewayne: Did anyone catch on?

Zina Garrison: My dentist knew. But I wouldn't listen to him. There was another problem. I was married then. My man kept telling me I was fat and ugly.

Kaleena: I hope you dumped him!

Zina Garrison: I did. But it took a while. I wanted to have kids. It was hard to let that go.

Bryce: How did you stop?

Zina Garrison: I had no choice. I kept winning for a while. Then I started losing. Everything. I lost my health. Then I lost my tennis games. I told John, my coach, what was going on. He got me to a doctor. Then I started seeing a therapist. That helped a lot.

Chandra: Do you diet now?

Zina Garrison: I watch what I eat. And I try to think about why I am eating. But I don't worry about my body so much. A big butt? So what. Much more fun to feel good than to have your head in a toilet.

Dewayne: *(laughing)* Thanks for that image!

Chandra: Are you going to play any more tennis?

Zina Garrison: Tennis? How about right now?

Narrator 1: As they head for the courts, Zina thinks about her mama. She knows that her mama would be proud of her for winning so much. Especially for winning back her health.

 **Cross Outs**

Zina Garrison

	A	B	C
1	thin hair	diabetes	win
2	soft nails	the	game
3	with	good	bulimia
4	health	Wimbledon	U.S. Open

1. Cross out the name of Zina's mama's disease in column B.

2. Cross out the names of 2 tennis competitions in row 4.

3. Cross out the name of Zina's secret in row 3.

4. Cross out 2 problems bulimia causes in column A.

Write the remaining words in order below.

_____ _____ _____ _____

_____ _____.

Tracey Gold

Actress

Summary

During the late 1980s and early 1990s, Tracey Gold co-starred in the sitcom *Growing Pains*. (The show is still seen in reruns on national cable stations.) Gold played the brainy teenager Carol Seaver. The show followed an American family as it faced the challenges of everyday life.

Gold was born in 1969. She had appeared in TV commercials, shows, and movies since the age of four. By age twelve, though, she faced a big problem. Doctors found that Gold suffered from anorexia nervosa. The disease is an eating disorder that causes those who have it to starve themselves—sometimes to death. The problem returned in Gold's late teens, at the height of *Growing Pains'* popularity. Quickly, Gold's weight dropped to dangerous lows.

Gold took a long and difficult road back to recovery. Later, she went on to star in dozens of TV movies. More important to her, though, was her marriage and the birth of her two children—something she once feared might never happen because of her battle with anorexia.

Presentation Suggestions

Before reading the play, students can do research on eating disorders such as anorexia and bulimia. After reading the play, students and teachers can look at pictures of female stars of today's hit TV shows. They can then talk about how their body images might affect their viewers and the thoughts that viewers have toward their own bodies.

Related Books and Media

- Gold, Tracey, and Julie McCarron. *Room to Grow: An Appetite for Life*. Beverly Hills, CA: New Millennium Press, 2003.

- Hornbacher, Marya. *Wasted: A Memoir of Anorexia and Bulimia*. New York: HarperCollins, 1998.

- Eating disorders: www.kidshealth.org/teen/

Characters

Narrator 1

Narrator 2

Tracey Gold, *a teenage actress*

Alan Thicke, *an actor*

Joanna Kerns, *an actress*

Kirk Cameron, *a teenage actor*

Director

Gene, *a TV producer*

Phil, *a TV producer*

Bonnie Gold, *Tracey's mother*

Tracey Gold
Actress

Scene 1

Narrator 1: The year is 1991. On a soundstage in California, the cast of the TV series *Growing Pains* runs through a scene. One of the characters, Carol Seaver (played by actress Tracey Gold), argues with her parents, Jason (Alan Thicke) and Maggie (Joanna Kerns). Also in the scene is Carol's brother, Mike (Kirk Cameron).

Tracey Gold: *(as Carol Seaver)* Mom, Dad, this isn't fair! You let Mike use the car as soon as he got his license! I have my license. Why can't I use the car?

Alan Thicke: *(as Jason)* This is completely different.

Tracey Gold: Why?

Alan Thicke: Because . . . because . . . why is it different, Maggie?

Joanna Kearns: *(as Maggie)* Because . . . I don't know why. It just is. That's all.

Kirk Cameron: *(as Mike)* It's a well-known fact that men are better drivers than women. Sorry, Carol. You'll have to find a new way to get to the dork convention.

Narrator 2: The studio audience laughs.

Tracey Gold: Keep that up, and you'll have to find a new way to walk.

Narrator 1: The audience laughs again. A director calls out from one side of the set.

Director: Cut! Great job, everybody. OK, let's take five.

Tracey Gold: *(to Kirk)* You know, I could really take you if I had to.

Kirk Cameron: We should save that for a special episode: Carol vs. Mike in a steel cage match.

Narrator 2: The two laugh. Gene, one of the show's producers, steps on to the set.

Gene: Tracey, can we have a word with you?

Tracey Gold: Sure.

Narrator 1: The two join Phil, another producer, on a corner of the set.

Tracey Gold: What's up?

Gene: This is a very touchy subject. We don't want to hurt your feelings.

Phil: Kirk has become quite a teen idol. You know that, right?

Tracey Gold: Of course. I see the mobs of girls at the studio gate every day.

Gene: Great. We want you to be just as popular with young guys. I mean, you're smart. You're funny. You're very pretty.

Tracey Gold: *(confused)* Well . . . thanks. But—

Phil: It's just that . . . you've put on a little weight lately.

Tracey Gold: *(stunned)* I have?

Gene: Yeah. It's no big deal. But we'd like you to lose a few pounds. It would really help your look on screen.

Tracey Gold: Oh. I see.

Phil: Again, I hope we didn't hurt your feelings.

Tracey Gold: No. Not at all. I'll try.

Gene: Great. Thanks, Tracey.

Tracey Gold: Excuse me.

Narrator 2: Tracey walks off the set.

Phil: I think she took that well.

Gene: Yeah, she's a sweet kid. Listen, tell the writers that Mike should make some "fat jokes" about Carol. Maybe that'll help give her some incentive.

Narrator 1: Meanwhile, Tracey enters her dressing room. Nervously, she looks at herself in the mirror. She turns from side to side. She begins to tremble. Her eyes fill with tears.

Scene 2

Narrator 2: Tracey sees a doctor. He places her on a diet. She loses twenty pounds quickly. People admire her new look.

Narrator 1: As time passes, the attention gives Tracey a new sense of power. She keeps dieting. Soon, she hardly eats at all.

Narrator 2: One day, Alan and Joanna are having lunch in the studio cafeteria.

Alan Thicke: Yes, I've noticed it. But I don't know what to do.

Joanna Kerns: Should we say something?

Alan Thicke: Well, if any of us is going to, it has to be you.

Joanna Kerns: Okay, I will.

Narrator 1: Just then, Tracey walks to the table. She wears a baggy sweater. She carries a salad and a small order of chicken.

Tracey Gold: Hi, guys! Can I join you?

Joanna Kerns: Sure, honey.

Alan Thicke: I was just leaving.

Narrator 2: Alan gives Joanna a look as he gets up to leave. Tracey sits across from Joanna.

Tracey Gold: So what's up?

Narrator 1: Joanna watches as Tracey cuts her chicken into very small pieces.

Joanna Kerns: Not much. Alan and I were just talking—about you, actually.

Tracey Gold: Really?

Narrator 2: Tracey takes one small bite of chicken. She then starts to cut up the lettuce in her salad.

Joanna Kerns: Yes. Tracey, we're worried about you.

Tracey Gold: Why?

Narrator 1: Tracey eats a small piece of lettuce.

Joanna Kerns: Honey. You've become way too thin.

Tracey Gold: *(laughing)* Is that all? Don't worry, Joanna. It's under control. I'm fine.

Joanna Kerns: You barely eat anything at all.

Tracey Gold: I'm eating now, aren't I?

Narrator 2: Tracey eats another tiny piece of lettuce.

Joanna Kerns: Look, I know this business can be hard on women. But you've got to take care of yourself.

Tracey Gold: You are *so sweet* to worry about me like this. But I feel great. Really.

Joanna Kerns: Tracey, I—

Tracey Gold: The second I feel like it's out of control, I'll see my doctor. I promise.

Joanna Kerns: I . . . I . . . all right. All right, Tracey.

Narrator 1: Joanna tries to smile.

Tracey Gold: *(getting up to leave)* I have to go—they're waiting for me in makeup.

Narrator 2: Joanna watches Tracey dump the rest of her lunch in the garbage. Then she leaves the room.

Scene 3

Narrator 1: Weeks later, Bonnie Gold, Tracey's mother, visits the set. She sees Kirk.

Bonnie Gold: Hi, Kirk. Is Tracey around?

Kirk Cameron: I haven't seen her.

Bonnie Gold: Oh. I'll wait for her here, then.

Kirk Cameron: Mrs. Gold . . . is Tracey all right?

Bonnie Gold: *(worried)* No, Kirk. She isn't. Her father and I . . . We don't know what to do for her anymore.

Kirk Cameron: Listen, I should tell you—I've heard rumors. They're thinking about taking Tracey off the show.

Bonnie Gold: Oh, no . . .

Kirk Cameron: That's the least of her problems, though. She needs to get her health back. If there's anything *we* can do—

Bonnie Gold: No, Kirk. She has to do this herself.

Narrator 2: Bonnie goes to Tracey's dressing room. She knocks on the door.

Bonnie Gold: Tracey? Are you in there?

Narrator 1: Bonnie steps into the room. There, Tracey is dressed in a halter-top and shorts. She looks at herself in the mirror.

Narrator 2: Her mother is shocked at the sight. Tracey's ribs stick out, and her arms and legs are little more than flesh and bones. Dark circles show under her eyes.

Tracey Gold: *(shakily)* Mom . . . ?

Bonnie Gold: Oh, Tracey . . .

Tracey Gold: Mom . . . what have I done to myself?

Narrator 1: Bonnie takes Tracey in her arms. Tracey bursts into tears.

Bonnie Gold: Tracey, listen. The doctor says you're down to 80 pounds. He says your heart rate is too high. You can damage your body if you keep this up. You can ruin your chances of having children. You could die. Do you want that?

Tracey Gold: No! No. I . . . I just want to get this under control. But I don't know how . . .

Bonnie Gold: You've got to get better, Tracey. I'm not going to lose you.

Tracey Gold: All right, mom. I will. I'll get better.

Scene 4

Narrator 2: Tracey sees another doctor. She is treated for anorexia nervosa. The disease is a mental illness that forces people to starve themselves. Slowly, Tracey begins to overcome the illness. In a few months, her weight is up to 95 pounds. That's about ten pounds lower than her ideal weight.

Narrator 1: In the meantime, she takes a long break from the show's final season. Still, she returns for the last shows. After *Growing Pains,* she is healthy enough to star in TV movies. In one, she plays a woman who has anorexia.

Narrator 2: In 1994, Tracey marries her longtime boyfriend. She has two children. Tracey continues acting. She also speaks to groups about anorexia.

Narrator 1: It is a March day in 2002. Tracey speaks to a group of college students.

Tracey Gold: Today, my weight stays between 105 and 110 pounds. It's still a constant battle, though. Sometimes, I can see all the things I've ever wanted slipping away from me. But I have to do everything I can to stay healthy. Not just for me, but for my children, too.

Narrator 2: Tracey pauses and looks at the crowd.

Tracey Gold: Between five and ten million girls in America have anorexia nervosa. About a million men have it, too. I don't have all the answers. But for anyone fighting this disease, I hope it's helpful to know that there's someone else who went through it. And it turned out all right.

Cross Outs

Tracey Gold

	A	B	C
1	Kirk	marriage	Alan
2	Growing	good	health
3	eating	is	doctor
4	a	children	treasure

1. Cross out the word that comes from the title of Tracey's show in column A.

2. Cross out the type of disorder Tracey had in row 3.

3. Cross out the names of two of Tracey's co-stars in row 1.

4. Cross out the kind of person who takes care of sick people in column C.

5. Cross out the two things most important to Tracey in column B.

Write the remaining words in order below.

_____ _____ _____ _____

_____ .

Bethany Hamilton

Surfer

Summary

Bethany Hamilton was born in Hawaii. By the time she was a toddler, her parents had her on a surfboard. At age eight, she was surfing competitively. At thirteen, she was projected as a future national champion.

But in 2003, Bethany suffered an accident that would forever change her life. That day, she was attacked by a tiger shark estimated to be fourteen feet long. The shark took her left arm, and only quick action by a family friend and the work of local doctors saved her life.

Her love of surfing, however, was not affected by the attack, and within a month, Bethany was back riding the waves. Weeks later, she resumed her competitive career, and later, she secured a spot for herself as a member of the U.S. National Surfing team.

Today, in addition to competitive surfing, Hamilton is also a motivational speaker. Among her audiences have been soldiers who have lost limbs in combat in Iraq.

Presentation Suggestions

Before reading the play, students might learn more about sharks and the relative frequency (or infrequency) of shark attacks in the United States. They can create and analyze a map of reported shark attacks in the United States and research whether sharks pose as great a danger to humans as people assume. They could also research and learn more about Hawaii and about the sport of competitive surfing.

Related Books and Media

- Lake, Sanoe. *Surfer Girl: A Guide to the Surfing Life*. New York: Little, Brown Young Readers, 2005.

- Llewellyn, Claire. *The Best Book of Sharks*. Boston: Kingfisher/Houghton Mifflin, 2005.

- Peterson, Christine. *Extreme Surfing*. Mankato, MN: Capstone Press, 2005.

- Bethany Hamilton: www.bethanyhamilton.com

Characters

Narrator 1	Alana Blanchard, *Bethany's friend*
Narrator 2	Holt Blanchard, *Alana's father*
Captain Walters	Doctor
Soldier 1	Tom Hamilton, *Bethany's father*
Soldier 2	Reporter
Bethany Hamilton	NSSA Judge, *a judge at a surfing competition*

Bethany Hamilton Surfer

Scene 1

Narrator 1: It's a spring afternoon in 2005. A group of soldiers are at an American Army base in Ramstein, Germany. They gather in the lounge of a clinic.

Narrator 2: All of the soldiers have been wounded in combat. Many of them are missing arms or legs. Two politicians had spoken to the men.

Narrator 1: Captain Walters stands at the front of the room.

Captain Walters: All right, men, listen up. I'm sure you want to join me in thanking our guests for visiting us today. I know they would have liked to have stayed longer.

Soldier 1: Yeah, they were a real shot in the arm. So to speak.

Captain Walters: You got a problem, soldier?

Soldier 2: I have one, sir. It's fine to have these big shots visit us. But what do they have to say? What do they know about what we've been through—or what we're going through now?

Soldier 1: He's right. I lost my arm last month, and I'm never getting it back. What's some politician going to say to make it better?

Captain Walters: Well, you may be right. But we have one speaker left today who you may find a bit more interesting. Gentlemen, let me introduce to you Miss Bethany Hamilton.

Narrator 2: A girl steps to the front of the room. She is fifteen years old. She is small, but looks fit. She is shy in front of the room of soldiers.

Bethany Hamilton: Um . . . hi guys.

Soldier 2: We can't hear you!

Bethany Hamilton: Sorry. Uh . . . hi. It's, uh . . . it's good to see you all. Thanks for coming out to see me.

Narrator 1: Bethany slips off her jacket. All of the men gasp when they see that she is missing her left arm.

Soldier 1: Hey, I know you! I heard about you on the news!

Soldier 2: Yeah, you're the surfer girl, aren't you?

Bethany Hamilton: Yeah, that's me. Um . . . I had a speech. But I forgot to bring it. *(the men chuckle)* Maybe if you guys have some questions, we could just talk.

Soldier 1: Well, uh . . . I have a question. Are you afraid of the ocean?

Soldier 2: How big was the shark?

Soldier 1: Did it . . . did it hurt much?

Captain Walters: Whoa, guys. Too many questions at once. Bethany, maybe you could just tell us your story.

Bethany Hamilton: Sure. It started out a few years ago. A bunch of years ago, in fact . . .

Scene 2

Bethany Hamilton: I grew up on Kauai. It's one of the islands of Hawaii. I've been surfing ever since I was a toddler. By the time I was seven years old, I was surfing without any help. By the time I was eight, I was surfing in competitions. I loved it. I knew that was what I wanted to do with my life.

Alana Blanchard: Come on, Bethany! Grab your board and let's go! My father's taking us down to the beach!

Bethany Hamilton: I was thirteen years old, and it was Halloween. My best friend Alana and I were going surfing with her dad. The water was clear that day. No sign of any trouble at all.

Alana Blanchard: So which competition is this again?

Bethany Hamilton: It's called the National Scholastic Surfing Association meet. It's being held over on the Big Island, at Banyans. I'll be in the Open Women Division. I think I can do pretty well. I think I can—whoa!

Alana Blanchard: Bethany? Bethany! What is it?

Narrator: Bethany, telling her story to the soldiers, pauses for a moment. They are hanging on her every word.

Bethany Hamilton: My left arm was hanging in the water. The shark came up out of nowhere. We think it was a tiger shark, about fourteen feet long. It grabbed on, and shook me back and forth. All I saw was a big gray blur. I just held onto the board with my right arm. Then it let go.

Alana Blanchard: Bethany! What's happening?

Bethany Hamilton: A shark . . . a shark bit me!

Alana Blanchard: Oh, no! Dad! Dad, help! Help!

Bethany Hamilton: Alana's father was nearby.

Holt Blanchard: Bethany! Oh no! Her arm! It's gone!

Alana Blanchard: Dad, what should we do?

Holt Blanchard: We have to stop the bleeding. I'll tie a tourniquet with this surfboard leash. You run for help. Get an ambulance! Hurry!

Scene 3

Bethany: If it weren't for Alana and her dad, I might have bled to death right there. It didn't seem like more than a few minutes passed before I was on my way to the hospital. My dad was already there. He was having knee surgery.

Doctor: This should be routine, Mr. Hamilton. Knee surgeries are pretty common nowadays. We'll have you up and moving around in no time.

Tom Hamilton: I hope so. My daughter is competing in a big surf meet in a couple of months. I was hoping to be up and around by then.

Doctor: No problem. You should be fine.

Nurse: *(bursting into the room)* Doctor, we have an emergency coming in. The paramedics are calling from the ambulance. You'd better take this call!

Doctor: Mr. Hamilton, if you'll excuse me.

Narrator 2: A moment later, the doctor rushes back into the operating room. A team of nurses follow him.

Doctor: *(barking orders)* All right, we're going to be dealing with lots of blood loss. I want six units of whole blood in here. Have six more ready.

Tom Hamilton: Doctor, what is it? What's going on?

Doctor: I'm sorry, Mr. Hamilton. Your knee is going to have to wait. We have an emergency coming in. I need this room.

Tom Hamilton: What is it? What happened?

Doctor: A surfer was attacked by a shark. She lost her arm.

Tom Hamilton: A surfer? You said, "she"? Who is it?

Doctor: We'll have time to talk later, Mr. Hamilton. Right now, I need to prepare this room.

Tom Hamilton: Doctor, you have to tell me! Was it Bethany?

Doctor: Mr. Hamilton, I . . . . Yes. Yes, it was. We're going to do all we can to help her.

Tom Hamilton: No! Not my daughter! Bethany!

Scene 4

Bethany Hamilton: By the time I got out of surgery, my story was making the news. Everyone in the country heard about me.

Doctor: *(speaking to the media)* Bethany has lost her left arm. She had lost 70 percent of her body's blood. Fortunately, it was a clean amputation, just below the shoulder. She was in such good shape. Otherwise, the blood loss alone could have killed her. She should make a full recovery.

Reporter: Doctor, what kind of life should she be able to lead?

Doctor: Well, right now, I don't see any other problems. She should be able to lead the normal life of any amputee.

Bethany Hamilton: The doctor was right. But "normal" to me meant surfing. I was back in the water within a month. I think that first ride on my new board was the hardest I ever took in my life.

Tom Hamilton: *(on the beach, watching Bethany surf)* Bethany! Bethany, you did it! How did it feel?

Bethany Hamilton: I'm—I'm okay, Dad. It was kind of hard getting up on the board, but once I did, it felt okay. It felt . . . great. I'm so glad to be back out here!

Tom Hamilton: You looked great, sweetheart. We're so proud of you!

Bethany Hamilton: By the time the big competition came up, I was anxious to go.

NSSA Judge: Bethany, are you sure you're ready for this? After all, it's only been ten weeks since your . . . since the accident.

Bethany Hamilton: I'm ready. I want to do this.

NSSA Judge: If you want, I could give you more time between heats. Or I could put you in a different heat. You could compete against surfers who aren't quite so experienced.

Bethany: No. Treat me like everyone else.

NSSA Judge: All right, Bethany. Go ahead and head out into the water. Good luck. I know you have a lot of people pulling for you.

Scene 5

Soldier 2: So . . . did you win the meet?

Bethany Hamilton: *(smiling)* No. I placed fifth in my age group. But considering what I had gone through, I thought it was a good start.

Captain Walters: Bethany can teach us all quite a lesson, men. She looked into the jaws of the beast. She won her battle.

Bethany Hamilton: Well, I don't know about that. The way I see it, this was just the plan for my life. I'm still a competitive surfer. I still want to win a world championship someday. But if I can talk to people—people like you guys—and help them as well. That makes life even better.

Narrator 1: The soldiers give Bethany a round of applause.

Bethany Hamilton: Never give up. People can do whatever they set their hearts to do. Just never give up. Just go out there and do it.

Cross Outs

Bethany Hamilton

	A	B	C
1	have	wave	shark
2	hospital	teenager	faith
3	in	soldier	islands
4	your	reporter	abilities

1. Cross out the name of what a surfer rides on in row 1.

2. Cross out the name of an animal that lives in the water in column C.

3. Cross out the name of the place where the sick and injured are treated in row 2.

4. Cross out the term for a person age 13 through 19 in column B.

5. Cross out the term describing a member of the Army in column B.

6. Cross out the name of the land masses that make up the state of Hawaii in column C.

7. Cross out the word in Row 4 that describes someone who works for a newspaper.

Write the remaining words in order below.

_____ _____ _____ _____

_____.

Carolyn McCarthy

Congresswoman

Summary

Congresswoman Carolyn McCarthy never planned to enter politics. A nurse, she lived a quiet, happy life in Mineola, New York. But on December 7, 1993, her world was torn apart. On that night, a gunman opened fire on a carload of people on a commuter train. Carolyn's husband, Dennis, was killed. Her son was gravely injured. In the months and years following the incident, Carolyn spoke out often against gun violence. Furious with her congressman's vote on a gun issue, Carolyn decided to run for the office herself. She won the election. At the time of this writing, she has been reelected three times. As a congresswoman, Carolyn has won many national awards for her work. She is widely admired as an ordinary citizen who beat the odds and devoted her life to helping people.

Presentation Suggestions

Before reading the play, students can use the Internet to find their congressional representatives. They can see where these officials stand on important issues. Students can also discuss which issues they would like to speak out on if they were elected to Congress.

Related Books and Media

- Catrow, David. *We the Kids: The Preamble to the United States Constitution*. New York: Dial Books, 2002.

- Sobel, Syl, and Pam Tanzey. *How the U.S. Government Works*. New York: Barrons Juvenile, 1999.

- Web Site of Congresswoman Carolyn McCarthy: http://carolynmccarthy.house.gov/

Characters

Narrator 1

Narrator 2

Carolyn McCarthy

Tom Cook, *Carolyn's brother*

Detective

Doctor

Dan Frisa, *a congressman from McCarthy's district*

Reporter 1

Reporter 2

Carolyn McCarthy
Congresswoman

Scene 1

Narrator 1: It is December 7, 1993. Carolyn McCarthy has spent the evening at a Christmas concert. She is driving to her home in Mineola, New York.

Carolyn McCarthy: I hope Dennis and Kevin got the tree set up.

Narrator 2: She pulls into the driveway. The Christmas tree sits by the garage. Carolyn's brother Tom stands in front of the house.

Carolyn McCarthy: Tom, what are you doing here? Where are Dennis and Kevin? They said they'd set up the tree as soon as they got home from work.

Tom Cook: They were . . . they were on the train.

Carolyn McCarthy: *(annoyed)* Of course they were. They're on the train every day. They work together.

Tom Cook: Didn't you hear?

Carolyn McCarthy: Hear what?

Tom Cook: Carolyn . . . something happened. Dennis is dead. Kevin is badly hurt. They don't think he's going to make it.

Carolyn McCarthy: *(stunned)* What are you saying?

Tom Cook: I'm sorry . . .

Narrator 1: Carolyn sits down on her front porch.

Carolyn McCarthy: Dennis . . . Kevin . . . oh, no. Oh, no!

Narrator 2: Carolyn begins to cry. After five minutes, though, she pulls herself together.

Carolyn McCarthy: *(choking back tears)* All right. Enough. We have to get to the hospital.

Narrator 1: Soon, they arrive at the hospital. They wait to hear from a doctor. In the meantime, a detective explains what happened.

Detective: Everything was normal on the train. Then this man got up. He had a gun. He began shooting everywhere. Your husband and son were hit pretty bad.

Carolyn McCarthy: Don't hold back, detective. I want to know everything.

Detective: Your husband was dead at the scene. He was found slumped over your son. Your son had been shot in the head.

Carolyn McCarthy: How can someone do this?

Detective: The gunman bought his gun legally in California. But it's illegal to carry it in New York. The clip he used to reload carries fifteen bullets. The bullets were specially designed to do as much damage as possible. Some other passengers tackled the guy while he was reloading. Here is what gets me, though. If the clip had carried fewer bullets, the guy might not have been able to shoot as many people as he did.

Narrator 2: A doctor arrives to talk to Carolyn.

Doctor: Mrs. McCarthy? You can come in and see Kevin for a moment.

Narrator 1: Kevin, age twenty-six, lies in a hospital bed. Much of his head is bandaged. Tubes run in and out of his body.

Doctor: Mrs. McCarthy, I know you're a nurse. I'll give it to you straight. Kevin was shot in the head. Much of his brain was exposed. Some of it still has bullet and bone pieces in it. He only has a 10 percent chance of living. And even then, he might be paralyzed. He could be a vegetable.

Narrator 2: Carolyn takes her son's hand.

Carolyn McCarthy: No. You're wrong. I've already lost my husband. I'm not losing my son. Kevin will live. And he'll move.

Scene 2

Narrator 1: Carolyn devotes herself to her son's recovery. He undergoes many months of surgery and rehabilitation. His hand and arm remain partly paralyzed. But he learns to walk again.

Narrator 2: Carolyn also becomes a public voice against gun violence. She speaks at rallies. She is interviewed on TV. She is also interviewed for newspapers and magazines. She helps lobby for a national law against assault weapons.

Carolyn McCarthy: *(to an interviewer)* I'm not going for a ban on guns. I'm not against hunting rifles and things like that. But why do regular citizens need assault weapons? Why are these weapons so easy to get?

Narrator 1: The law is passed, thanks to Carolyn's help. The gunman from the train is found guilty of his crimes. Carolyn is one of the victims' family members who speaks to the gunman in court before his sentencing.

Carolyn McCarthy: *(to the gunman)* I will give you no hatred. I will give you none of my rage. You are an evil person, so you are not worthy of my time or thoughts. You are not worthy of my energy. You are going to prison. You will never see the light of day again. Your justice is about to be served.

Narrator 2: Carolyn pauses for a moment.

Carolyn McCarthy: You took away my husband. But you will never take away my memory of him. You will be gone from my thoughts forever. And we will learn to love and laugh again.

Narrator 1: The gunman is sentenced to more than 300 years in prison.

Scene 3

Narrator 2: Soon Carolyn hears some bad news. Some members of Congress plan to repeal the assault-gun law she had fought so hard to pass. Carolyn goes to Washington, D.C. She speaks with the congressman from her district. His name is Dan Frisa.

Carolyn McCarthy: How can you vote for this repeal? The railroad shooting took place in your own district!

Dan Frisa: I'm sorry, Carolyn. But I think the assault-gun bill is a bad law.

Carolyn McCarthy: Is that so? Well, I think you're being controlled by your political party and the pro-gun lobbyists. You have to stand up for what's right!

Dan Frisa: That's what I'm doing. Now if you'll excuse me, Carolyn. I have a lot of work to do.

Carolyn McCarthy: *(stopping him)* Wait just one minute. You listen to me, Congressman. If you vote for this repeal, I'll do everything in my power to make sure you don't get reelected. I'll—I'll run for the office myself if I have to!

Dan Frisa: Carolyn, I know that this is a very emotional issue for you. And I'm sorry for what you've gone through. But my mind is made up.

Narrator 1: Frisa casts his vote. The repeal fails in Congress. Carolyn keeps her promise.

Scene 4

Narrator 2: It is September 1996. Carolyn stands on a platform in front of her house. Kevin is still partially paralyzed. Still, he stands by her side. A throng of reporters crowd in front of her.

Narrator 1: The street is filled with her neighbors and supporters. They wave signs reading "McCarthy for Congress," and "Go, Carolyn, Go!"

Carolyn McCarthy: My name is Carolyn McCarthy. And I am running for Congress.

Narrator 2: The crowd goes wild. The cameras flash over and over again.

Carolyn McCarthy: This journey started on December 7, 1993. That day changed my life forever. Today begins the newest step. I want to make sure that no family has to go through what we went through.

Reporter 1: Mrs. McCarthy, do you think you're ready to handle complex issues like the federal budget?

Carolyn McCarthy: Look, we all have budgets. The only difference with this one is that there are more zeros in it.

Narrator 1: The crowd laughs.

Carolyn McCarthy: But I know about other issues. I'm a nurse and a mother. I know about health care. I know about education. And I want to learn as much as I can.

Reporter 2: Politics can be a rough business. Can you handle it? Would you even have gone into politics if not for this terrible tragedy?

Narrator 2: The smile disappears from Carolyn's face.

Carolyn McCarthy: No, I wouldn't. Absolutely not. *(pausing)* I'm a nurse. When I was a teenager, my boyfriend was in a bad car accident. He died. I wanted to do something about that. As a nurse, I took on patients no one else would touch. Burn victims. The terminally ill.

Narrator 1: The crowd is silent. They hang on her every word.

Carolyn McCarthy: If I could face all that, I think I can handle politics.

Narrator 2: The race for Congress becomes one of the most closely watched in the country. During the race, Frisa keeps a low profile.

Dan Frisa: *(to a reporter)* Carolyn McCarthy has only one issue to stand on: gun control. And she's wrong about it.

Scene 5

Narrator 1: It is election night, 1996. Carolyn takes the stage at a hotel ballroom in Mineola. The room is packed with her cheering supporters. They chant, "CAR-O-LYN! CAR-O-LYN!" TV camera lights glare on the podium.

Narrator 2: Carolyn smiles and waves at the crowd. She hugs Kevin before stepping to the microphone.

Carolyn McCarthy: My friends, Dan Frisa just called to congratulate me. In January, I'm going to Washington, D.C. I'll be sworn in as your new congresswoman.

Narrator 1: The crowd goes wild with celebration. It's several minutes before Carolyn can speak again.

Carolyn McCarthy: I want to thank all of you for your help. All we wanted to do was make something good come out of a horrible situation. Well, I think we did that.

Narrator 2: As of this writing, Carolyn McCarthy still serves as congresswoman from the Fourth District of New York. She has fought for the economy and for education. She has fought for keeping guns out of schools and away from criminals.

 **Cross Outs**

Carolyn McCarthy

	A	B	C
1	overcome	Washington, D.C.	tragedy
2	Mineola	assault	and
3	health care	find	education
4	New York	success	federal budget

1. Cross out the name of our nation's capital in column B.

2. Cross out the kind of guns Carolyn McCarthy fights against in row 2.

3. Cross out the city and state Carolyn McCarthy represents in column A.

4. Cross out the two issues Carolyn McCarthy says she knows about in row 3.

5. Cross out the issue Carolyn McCarthy is asked about in column C.

Write the remaining words in order below.

_____ _____ _____ _____

_____.

Tim McGraw

Country Singer

Summary

By age twenty-seven, Tim McGraw was a huge country music star. In fact, his life could have been the subject of a country song. Tim's family grew up poor in a small town in Louisiana. Times were so hard that the family moved thirteen times during Tim's childhood. "These places, I'd fix them up and make them home," his mother, Betty, said. "But in some, you could see the dirt on the ground through the floor."

When he was eleven years old, Tim discovered a family secret that was to change his life forever. Tim found out he was the son of major-league baseball player Tug McGraw. Tug was as well known for his offbeat sense of humor as he was for the great screwball that made him a top relief pitcher for the New York Mets and the Philadelphia Phillies. It took years for Tim to overcome feelings of anger and abandonment toward his biological father. Eventually, the two formed a special bond. "We've become like older and younger brothers," Tim said. "Me being the older brother and him being the younger brother is what it's come down to."

Presentation Suggestions

Before reading the play, students can research the careers of both Tug and Tim McGraw. Sports paraphernalia can be gathered for the reading.

Related Books and Media

- Gray, Scott. *Perfect Harmony: The Faith Hill and Tim McGraw Story.* New York: Ballentine Books, 1999.

- McGraw, Tim. *Tim McGraw and the Dancehall Doctors: This Is Ours.* New York: Atria Books, 2002.

- Tim's official Web site: www.timmcgraw.com

Characters

Narrator 1

Narrator 2

Sandy Smith, *Tim McGraw's sister*

Tim Smith (later Tim McGraw)

Betty Smith, *Tim's mother*

Tug McGraw, *baseball player*

Diner cashier

Photographer

Tim McGraw
Country Singer

Scene 1

Narrator 1: It is 1978 in Start, Louisiana. Eleven-year-old Tim Smith is taping baseball cards to his bedroom wall. His sister Sandy looks in the door.

Sandy Smith: You're not supposed to do that. Mom said the tape leaves marks on the walls.

Tim Smith: She said I could hang up a few. I just got these.

Sandy Smith: Who are they?

Tim Smith: This one's George Brett. That one's Dwight Evans. And that's Tug McGraw. By the way, what time is Mom getting home?

Sandy Smith: About 5:30, I guess. Why?

Tim Smith: And Daddy's out on a trucking run. Want to check out Mom's closet? She's hiding our Christmas presents in there.

Sandy Smith: Tim Smith! Don't you dare! Mom will have a fit if she finds out.

Tim Smith: She won't—unless you tell her. Are you going to tattle on me?

Sandy Smith: Well, no. But . . .

Tim Smith: Good. Then I'm going for it. You want to know what you're getting?

Sandy Smith: No! Leave me out of this.

Narrator 2: Sandy leaves. Tim goes into his mother's room. He opens the closet door.

Tim Smith: Maybe she hid them in one of these boxes.

Narrator 1: Tim opens the first box. He begins searching.

Tim Smith: Nope. Just some old pictures and papers. Hey. What's this?

Narrator 2: Tim finds an envelope marked "Tim's Birth Certificate." He opens it and pulls out a piece of paper.

Tim Smith: Born May 1st, Delhi, Louisiana. Samuel Timothy . . . McGraw?

Narrator 1: Later that evening, Tim's mother comes home. She goes to her bedroom and turns on the light. She finds Tim sitting on her bed.

Betty Smith: Oh! Tim, you startled me. Why are you sitting in the dark?

Narrator 2: Tim looks shocked.

Betty Smith: Tim, what is it? Are you okay?

Tim Smith: I found my birth certificate. It says my name is McGraw, not Smith.

Betty Smith: Oh, dear. Tim, we wanted to wait until you were older to tell you.

Tim Smith: Tell me what?

Betty Smith: Well, back in the summer of 1966, I was in love with a minor-league baseball player. He's your birth father. I didn't tell anyone because I didn't want to hurt his career. Later, Horace and I got married. We decided it would be best for him to raise you as his son.

Tim Smith: Does my father know about me?

Betty Smith: Yes, he knows.

Tim Smith: Do I ever get to meet him?

Betty Smith: Maybe. We'll have to check his team's schedule.

Tim Smith: You mean he's still playing baseball? Who is he?

Betty Smith: His name is Tug. Tug McGraw.

Narrator 1: Tim stares at his mother in shock.

Betty Smith: Have you heard of him?

Scene 2

Narrator 2: Betty gets in touch with Tug. A few weeks later, Tim and his mother drive to Houston, Texas. The Philadelphia Phillies are playing the Houston Astros.

Narrator 1: After the game, Betty and Tim wait outside the players' entrance. Finally, Tug McGraw steps out.

Betty Smith: Hi, Tug.

Tug McGraw: Hi, Betty. How have you been?

Betty Smith: I've been good.

Narrator 2: An awkward moment passes.

Betty Smith: Tug, this is . . . this is Tim. Tim, this is . . . your father.

Narrator 1: Tug holds out his hand.

Tug McGraw: Nice to meet you, Tim.

Narrator 2: Tim pauses a moment. He shakes Tug's hand.

Tim Smith: Hi.

Tug McGraw: I guess you have a lot of questions.

Tim Smith: No. Mom told me what happened.

Tug McGraw: I know this must be a shock. I'm very sorry for that.

Tim Smith: It's okay.

Narrator 2: Again, there is a moment of awkward silence.

Tug McGraw: I wish I could stay and talk. But the team bus is heading for the airport in a few minutes.

Betty Smith: It's okay. Take care of yourself, Tug.

Tug McGraw: You too, Betty. So long, Tim. It was good to meet you.

Narrator 1: Tim doesn't say anything. Finally, Tug walks away. Betty puts her arm around Tim's shoulder.

Betty Smith: All right, honey. Let's go home.

Narrator 2: For the next seven years, Tim doesn't hear from his father.

Scene 3

Narrator 1: It is April 1986. Tim is now eighteen years old. He sits in a diner outside Philadelphia, Pennsylvania.

Narrator 2: Soon, Tug enters. The man behind the cash register sees him.

Cashier: Hey! Aren't you Tug McGraw? From the Phillies?

Tug McGraw: That's right. But I don't play anymore.

Cashier: Still, you were my favorite player.

Tug McGraw: Thanks. That's kind of . . .

Narrator 1: Tug sees Tim sitting in the booth.

Tug McGraw: Would you excuse me? I'm meeting someone.

Cashier: No problem. Anything you need, you just ask.

Narrator 2: Tug walks over to Tim's booth. He sits down.

Tug McGraw: Tim, is that you? Wow! How you've grown!

Tim Smith: Yeah. Listen, I have to catch a bus back home soon. I don't have a lot of time.

Tug McGraw: Okay. What did you want to see me about?

Tim Smith: I want to go to college. But I can't pay for it. I need your help.

Tug McGraw: Okay. Sure. I guess it's the least I can do.

Tim Smith: Good. Thanks.

Narrator 1: The two say nothing for a moment.

Tug McGraw: Tim, listen. I know I've made some mistakes in my life. And I know that it's too late for me to be a father to you. But maybe I can be a friend.

Tim Smith: Okay. I guess we can try that.

Narrator 2: Tim begins college. He and Tug keep in touch. They spend time together. Meanwhile, Tim buys himself a used guitar for $20. He teaches himself to play. Soon, he's singing at local bars. He also begins using his real name: Tim McGraw.

Scene 4

Narrator 1: It is 1989. At a bar near Northeast Louisiana University, Tim finishes singing.

Tim McGraw: Thanks everyone. Goodnight!

Narrator 2: The audience cheers loudly for him. As Tim steps off the stage, he hears a familiar voice.

Tug McGraw: Not bad, kid. But you should hear your old man sing!

Tim McGraw: Tug! You made it! Let's go to the back room and talk.

Narrator 1: The two sit down to talk.

Tug McGraw: That was great, Tim. You have a lot of talent.

Tim McGraw: Thanks. Actually, that is what I wanted to talk to you about. Tug, I'm taking some time off from college. I'm going to Nashville. I want to be a musician.

Tug McGraw: No kidding? That's a big decision.

Tim McGraw: I know. Everyone thinks I'm crazy for doing it. So . . . what do you think?

Narrator 2: Tug thinks for a moment.

Tug McGraw: Tim, I saw you on that stage. I know where your heart is. I think you should go for it.

Tim McGraw: You do?

Tug McGraw: Yes. I know what it's like to live out a dream. Go to Nashville. Give it your best shot.

Narrator 1: In Nashville, Tim becomes a successful musician. In 1992, he gets a meeting with a record executive who was a big Tug McGraw fan.

Narrator 2: In 1993, Tim records his first album. His second album becomes a huge hit in 1994. Tim becomes one of country music's biggest stars.

Narrator 1: In 1996, Tim marries fellow country star Faith Hill. They have three daughters. Meanwhile, Tim and Tug continue to see each. They become a family.

Scene 5

Narrator 2: It is March 2001. Tim is in Florida to play in a charity softball game. He sees Tug on the field.

Tim McGraw: Hey, old-timer! How's the arm?

Tug McGraw: Tim! How are you? How are the kids?

Narrator 1: The two shake hands and hug each other.

Tim McGraw: Fantastic! They want to see you again.

Narrator 2: A news photographer sees the two men.

Photographer: Hey! It's Tim McGraw! Tim, can I get some pictures?

Tim McGraw: Sure, no problem.

Narrator 1: The photographer speaks to Tug.

Photographer: Hey, buddy. Can you step out of the way?

Narrator 2: Tim speaks to the news teams that are gathering.

Tim McGraw: Hey, everyone. This is my father, Tug McGraw.

Photographer: Didn't you used to pitch in the big leagues?

Tug McGraw: That's what they tell me.

Photographer: Are you both playing in the game today?

Tim McGraw: Yeah. We're on the same team.

Tug McGraw: I don't want him to embarrass me by getting a hit off of me.

Narrator 1: The photographers laugh.

Tim McGraw: Anything to keep peace in the family.

Cross Outs

Tim McGraw

	A	B	C
1	baseball	the	McGraws
2	softball	Philadelphia	Nashville
3	score	Faith Hill	big
4	pictures	hits	photographer

1. Cross out 2 names of sports in column A.

2. Cross out the names of 2 cities in row 2.

3. Cross out the name of a country singer in column B.

4. Cross out the word that means photos in row 4.

5. Cross out the word for someone who takes pictures in column C.

Write the remaining words in order below.

_____ _____ _____ _____

_____.

Willie O'Ree

Hockey Player

Summary

Willie O'Ree grew up in Canada where he learned ice-skating as a young boy. He joined a hockey team and dreamed of playing professionally. Willie O'Ree began to learn how difficult it could be to be a black person in a predominantly white world. Then he was dealt a huge blow when he lost sight in one eye during a game. He didn't let that hold him back, however, and continued to pursue playing professional hockey. Eventually, he was invited to play for the Boston Bruins, becoming the first African American in the National Hockey League.

Presentation Suggestions

The stage can have hockey equipment on it. A winter mural can decorate the back. Posters featuring hockey and Willie O'Ree can be displayed.

Related Book and Media

- Kaminsky, Marty. *Uncommon Champions: Fifteen Athletes Who Battled Back.* Honesdale, PA: Boyds Mills Press, 2000.

- Official Web Site of the National Hockey League: www.nhl.com

Characters

Narrator 1

Narrator 2

Willie O'Ree

Dad, *Willie O'Ree's father*

Joe McQuade, *barber*

Coach

Richard O'Ree, *Willie's brother*

Doctor

Scout

Milt Schmidt, *coach of the Boston Bruins*

Willie O'Ree
Hockey Player

Scene 1

Narrator 1: On a cold winter day in Fredericton, New Brunswick, Willie O'Ree calls to his dad.

Willie: Hurry up, Dad! I want to skate! I want to fly across the ice!

Mr. O'Ree: Hold on, son. You need to learn first.

Willie: I know I can skate, Dad. Just get them on.

Narrator 2: Mr. O'Ree straps on Willie's homemade skates. Each skate is a block of wood with two blades stuck on the bottom. Straps hold them in place on Willie's shoes.

Narrator 1: The ice rink is also homemade. Mr. O'Ree has flooded the back yard. The cold Canadian winter did the rest.

Dad: Willie, use this chair for balance. Just push it along in front of you. You'll get the hang of it.

Willie: Here I go!

Narrator 2: Willie takes a few tumbles, but before long he is flying across the ice. During the long winters he skates everywhere. Often he can skate to school on the frozen sidewalks.

Narrator 1: The O'Rees are one of only two black families in town. But Willie has lots of friends, and it's clear he's a good skater. By the time he turns five years old, Willie is playing on a hockey team. When he is thirteen, everyone knows he is a talented skater.

Scene 2

Narrator 2: Even though Fredericton is a good place to live, there are still places a black person can't go. One of those places is a white barbershop. Willie is friends with the barber's son. Mr. Joe McQuade cuts Willie's hair on his front porch.

Willie: Mr. McQuade, what would happen if I came into your shop for a haircut?

Mr. McQuade: I don't know. I haven't given it any thought.

Willie: Well, I have. I'm going to come in for a haircut.

Narrator 1: Willie does what he promised. When he walks into the shop, all four barber chairs are full. People are also waiting for their turn.

Narrator 2: Soon Willie's turn comes. One of the barbers looks at him.

Willie: I'm waiting for Mr. McQuade.

Narrator 1: Everyone in the shop is quiet. Mr. McQuade finishes the haircut. Willie sits down. He gets his haircut. He is just thirteen and has just broken his first color barrier.

Scene 3

Narrator 2: At age fifteen, Willie tries out for the high school team.

Coach: All right, O'Ree. Let's see what you can do.

Narrator 1: The coach's son skates toward Willie with the puck. He has his head down. Willie steps in front of him and knocks him down.

Coach: Hit the bench, O'Ree! *(to his son)* Son, are you okay?

Narrator 2: That night, Willie talks to his brother, Richard, who is in his twenties.

Richard: So, how did tryouts go?

Willie: I didn't make the team.

Richard: What? You're a great hockey player.

Willie: I stepped in front of the coach's son. He got a broken collarbone.

Richard: That's bad luck for both of you. But I heard that the Fredericton Junior Capitals are having tryouts. Give it a go!

Narrator 1: The Capitals are part of the Junior Hockey League. Willie makes the team. He shows that he's a great player. The high school coach sees him play and talks with him.

Coach: O'Ree, why don't you come back and play for me? Let's just say you had a bad day at tryouts.

Willie: Sorry, Coach. I think I'll just play with the Capitals.

Narrator 2: Willie plays with the Capitals for two years. He also plays baseball in the summer. He knows he is a good athlete and feels like he can do anything he wants to do.

Scene 4

Narrator 1: Willie dreams about playing in the big leagues for years. His brother thinks he has a chance.

Richard: You can do it, Willie. You can make it all the way.

Willie: Even to the National Hockey League? No black man has ever gotten in the NHL.

Richard: You could be the first then. What do you have to lose? You have the talent.

Narrator 2: Some coaches believe in Willie too. By the time he is twenty, he is playing for the Junior Canucks. Then Willie's career in hockey comes to a stop.

Narrator 1: During a game, a puck hits Willie just above his right eye. He is taken to the hospital where he is treated. The next morning, the doctor shares the bad news.

Doctor: Willie, you had a lot of injuries. Your nose and cheekbone are broken. Your face is cut up.

Willie: What about my eye? Why do I have a patch over it?

Doctor: There was a lot of damage. We couldn't fix it. I'm afraid you have lost the sight in your right eye.

Willie: Are you sure?

Doctor: Yes, son. There's nothing we can do for you. You'll never play hockey again.

Narrator 2: Willie can't get the doctor's words out of his head. But he decides to get back on the ice after he has healed.

Narrator 1: He also decides the doctor doesn't know everything. He decides not to tell anyone he is blind in one eye. He learns to turn his head to see the puck. And he finishes out the season playing hockey.

Narrator 2: At the end of the season, he is asked to play on the Aces, a team in Quebec. He is given $4,000 for the season. In 1956, that's a lot of money. It's also a lot of money for a twenty-year-old who is blind in one eye.

Scene 5

Narrator 1: Willie spends that summer playing baseball for the Marysville Royals. This helps him stay in shape. He also earns a bit of money.

Narrator 2: A scout for the Milwaukee Braves sees him play.

Scout: Mr. O'Ree, we'd like you to try out for the Braves at our training camp.

Willie: Baseball camp? I don't want to go to baseball camp. I like what I'm doing here. Besides, I'm going to be a hockey player.

Scout: What do you have to lose? Why don't you go and see what it's like?

Narrator 1: Willie decides to go. He flies to the camp in Atlanta. This is his first time in the south. He calls his brother to tell him about his first week.

Willie: Richard, you wouldn't believe this place.

Richard: Why? What's wrong?

Willie: They have washrooms for whites only and coloreds only.

Richard: Is that a fact?

Willie: Not only that, but the taxi driver took me to an all-black hotel. And I had to sit in the back of the bus.

Richard: What is it like at the camp?

Willie: They put all the black people together there too. I don't know what I'm doing here. I want to play pro hockey, not pro baseball.

Richard: What are you going to do? Come home?

Willie: No, I guess I'll stick it out. They'll probably cut me quickly anyway.

Narrator 1: Willie is right. After two weeks, Willie is cut from the team. He isn't sad, even though he sits at the back of a bus for three days to get home.

Scene 6

Narrator 2: Willie loves playing for the Quebec Aces. It isn't the NHL, but it is a good minor league hockey team. He travels all over Canada, playing hard.

Narrator 1: Willie scores twenty-two goals in his first season. The team makes the playoffs. They win the trophy. They are the best team in Canada.

Narrator 2: The Boston Bruins have a working agreement with the Aces. That means that the Bruins can invite players from the Aces to try out for them. One summer day in 1957, Willie comes home from his job at a gas station.

Richard: Willie, there's a letter here for you.

Willie: Who's it from?

Richard: The Boston Bruins. Open it!

Narrator 1: Willie opens the letter.

Richard: Well, what does it say?

Willie: They want me to report to their training camp in Boston in September!

Richard: Willie! You've made it! You're going to be playing for the Bruins!

Willie: I have to make the team still.

Richard: You'll make it. And you'll be the first black man in the NHL.

Narrator 2: Willie goes to camp with a teammate from the Aces, Stan Maxwell. Stan is also black. At the end of training camp, Coach Milt Schmidt calls in Willie and Stan.

Milt Schmidt: Fellows, you've done a good job. But you're not quite ready for the Bruins. Go home and play for a year. Then we'll talk again.

Narrator 1: Willie and Stan are disappointed. But they know that a lot of players don't make the team at first. Willie figures he just has to work harder. He goes back to playing for the Aces.

Narrator 2: In January of 1958, Willie gets a phone call from Coach Schmidt.

Schmidt: Willie, one of our players is injured. We need you for a couple of games. Can you meet us in Montreal?

Willie: I'll be there!

Narrator 1: Willie takes the train to Montreal. On January 18, 1958, he pulls on a brown-and-gold jersey with a big *B* on the front.

Narrator 2: Willie and the Bruins beat the Montreal Canadiens 3 to 0. Willie doesn't score any goals, but he reaches his biggest goal. He becomes the first black man to play in the NHL.

Cross Outs

Willie O'Ree

	A	B	C
1	NHL	hockey	baseball
2	players	reach	eye
3	Marysville	their	Atlanta
4	goals	Aces	collarbone

1. Cross out two body parts injured during the play in column C.
2. Cross out the name of pro hockey's "big leagues" in row 1.
3. Cross out the name of the other sport Willie plays in Column C.
4. Cross out the two cities where Willie plays the other sport in row 3.
5. Cross out the name of the hockey team Willie plays for in row 4.

Write the remaining words in order below.

_____ _____ _____ _____

_____.

Freddie Prinze Jr.

Actor

Summary

It's not easy to succeed in show business. Sometimes, being related to someone famous can help. But this was not the case for Freddie Prinze Jr. Prinze's father, Freddie Prinze Sr., was a stand-up comedian. He was a huge star by the time he was nineteen years old. He then starred in the hit TV show *Chico and the Man.* But by age twenty-two, Prinze's life was coming apart. He was using drugs. His marriage was failing. Finally, he shot and killed himself. Prinze's son, Freddie Jr., was only ten months old at the time. His mother moved Freddie Jr. out of Los Angeles, California. She raised him in Albuquerque, New Mexico. There, she hoped he could live a normal life.

But Freddie Jr. was an outcast in school. He created a make-believe world in which he was a superhero. Other kids teased and bullied him. What Freddie didn't know was that he was training himself for life as an actor.

After high school, he moved back to Los Angeles. Within a couple of years, he was starring in hit films such as *Boys and Girls, Summer Catch,* and *I Know What You Did Last Summer.* Freddie not only had to overcome the loss of his father, he also had to deal with the reaction of people in show business to his father's legacy. He has done both while becoming a major success.

Presentation Suggestions

Before reading the play, students can do research on the careers of Freddie Prinze Sr. and Freddie Prinze Jr. They can discuss the similarities and differences between the two men's careers.

Related Books and Media

- McCracken, Kristen. *Freddie Prinze Jr.* Danbury, CT: Children's Press, 2001.

- Wilson, Wayne and Barbara Mitchell. *Freddie Prinze Jr.* Bear, DE: Mitchell Lane, 2002.
- Freddie Prinze Jr.: www.freddieprinzejr.com

Characters

Narrator 1

Narrator 2

Freddie Prinze, *Freddie Prinze Jr.'s father*

Kathy Prinze, *Freddie Prinze Jr.'s mother*

Freddie Prinze Jr.

Ron Deblasio, *Freddie Prinze Jr.'s friend*

Nick, *student*

Mark, *student*

Al, *student*

Rachel Leigh Cook, *actress*

# Freddie Prinze Jr.
Actor

Scene 1

Narrator 1: It is January 1977. In a hotel suite in Los Angeles, Freddie Prinze sits on the edge of his bed. He is very upset. His wife, Kathy, stands before him.

Freddie Prinze Sr.: Baby, please. We can make this work. I know we can.

Kathy Prinze: No, Freddie, we can't. It's out of control. The drugs. The fans. Reporters hounding us all the time. I can't take it anymore.

Freddie Prinze Sr.: I can change, baby. I can get off drugs. We can go somewhere quiet. Just you, me, and Freddie Jr. I can give this all up.

Kathy Prinze: I've heard that a thousand times before, Freddie. Even if you can quit drugs, you'll never give up the rest of it. Show business is in your blood. But it's not in mine. Freddie Jr. is only ten months old. I don't want him growing up like this. I'm leaving, Freddie. I'm filing for divorce.

Freddie Prinze Sr: *(breaking down)* No. No . . . please don't. Don't leave me alone. Don't take my son . . . .

Kathy Prinze: I'm sorry, Freddie. Good luck. Take care of yourself.

Narrator 2: Kathy walks out the door. Freddie is too stunned to move. Finally, he gets up and walks across the room. He opens a dresser drawer and pulls out a pistol. He holds it in his hand while he stares into the mirror.

Scene 2

Narrator 1: It is a fall afternoon in 1987 in Albuquerque, New Mexico. Freddie Prinze Jr. is now twelve years old. He arrives home from school.

Kathy Prinze: Hi, sweetheart. How was your day?

Freddie Jr.: Same as always.

Kathy Prinze: I'm sorry, honey. It'll get better. I promise.

Freddie Prinze Jr.: The kids at school hate me. They call me "weirdo" and "moron," and stuff I can't even say to you. And they keep making fun of me because I don't have a father. What's up with that, Mom? Who is my father? Why don't I ever get to see him?

Kathy Prinze: Umm . . . you know, Uncle Ron is coming to see us tonight. Maybe . . . maybe he can explain it to you.

Narrator 2: Later, Ron Deblasio, a family friend, visits Kathy and Freddie. After dinner, Ron and Freddie talk in Freddie's room.

Ron Deblasio: Freddie, I hear you've been asking about your dad.

Freddie Prinze Jr.: Yeah. But Mom never wants to talk about him.

Ron Deblasio: It's not easy for her. But if you want, I'll tell you anything you want to know.

Freddie Prinze Jr.: Tell me about my father. Please.

Ron Deblasio: Freddie, your father was a comedian. A great one. He made a lot of people laugh. I was his manager, in fact.

Freddie Prinze Jr.: What happened to him?

Ron Deblasio: He became very famous at a young age. He didn't handle it well. He got involved with drugs. As fast as he made it to the top . . . well, he hit rock bottom just as fast. We all tried to help him, but he was very depressed. And one night . . . he shot and killed himself.

Freddie Prinze Jr.: No way . . .

Ron Deblasio: I'm sorry, Freddie.

Freddie Prinze Jr.: Why? Why did he do this? Wasn't I good enough for him to want to stay alive?

Ron Deblasio: It had nothing to do with you, Freddie. He loved you very much. He had a good heart. But his problems just seemed to overwhelm him. We'll never know what he was thinking. All we can do is go on with our own lives.

Narrator 1: Freddie sits on the bed, shocked and confused.

Scene 3

Narrator 2: Freddie has trouble dealing with the facts of his father's death. He withdraws from his peers even further. As he reaches high school, he is unpopular. He has few friends.

Narrator 1: Freddie is lonely and sad. He retreats into a fantasy world based on comic books. He sees himself as a superhero. He battles make-believe villains on the school's football field. Often, he is seen running and dodging energy blasts as he fights alongside fellow heroes.

Freddie Prinze Jr.: Pegasus, look out! Magnatron is loose! We have to focus our firepower on him! Now! Blast him!

Narrator 2: Across the field, a group of Freddie's classmates watch him.

Nick: Can you believe this?

Mark: The kid is out of his mind.

Al: Come on—let's see how he handles getting his butt kicked in the real world.

Narrator 1: Freddie doesn't see the boys approaching.

Freddie Prinze Jr.: Back off, Magnatron! You can't beat us all!

Nick: Hey, Super-dork!

Narrator 2: Freddie freezes in his tracks and faces the other kids.

Freddie Prinze Jr.: What do you want? Leave me alone!

Mark: We can't. Magnatron called us in for backup!

Narrator 1: Mark's friends laugh and push Freddie to the ground. They begin punching and kicking him.

Scene 4

Narrator 2: Finally, Freddie graduates from high school. Now eighteen, he must choose a career. He sits down with his mother to talk about it.

Kathy Prinze: You're going to do *what*?

Freddie Prinze Jr.: I'm moving to Los Angeles, Mom. I'm going to be an actor.

Kathy Prinze: Well . . . I can't say I'm happy about this.

Freddie Prinze Jr.: I didn't think you would be. But I don't have a lot of choices. My grades were bad. We have no money for college. The only thing I was good at in school was school plays. I have a strong imagination. I can do this.

Kathy Prinze: Freddie . . . your father—

Freddie Prinze Jr.: Mom, I'd never do what he did. I would never make my family feel sad like that.

Kathy Prinze: I know, Freddie. And I don't know if this is the right thing for you. But I'll always stand behind you. No matter what.

Narrator 1: Freddie moves to Los Angeles. He works in a restaurant to pay the rent for his one-room apartment. He takes acting classes at night. He goes to many auditions.

Narrator 2: Finally, he gets his first acting job. He has a guest-starring role on the TV show *Family Matters*. Soon, his acting ability and his good looks lead to more roles.

Narrator 1: Freddie lands parts in films such as *Boys and Girls*, *Summer Catch*, and *Down to You*. Once the high school nerd, Freddie is now a teen heartthrob. He is one of the hottest rising stars in Hollywood.

Narrator 2: In 1999, Freddie is on the set of the movie *She's All That*. In it, he plays a high school hunk who bets that he can turn a "nerdy" girl into a prom queen.

Narrator 1: He shoots the scene in which the girl finds out that he dated her as part of a bet. The actress is Rachel Leigh Cook. As soon as the scene finishes, he rushes off the set. Cook follows him to his dressing room.

Rachel Leigh Cook: Freddie? Is something wrong?

Freddie Prinze Jr.: *(on the verge of tears)* No. No, I'm okay. *(he breaks down crying)*

Rachel Leigh Cook: Freddie! What is it? What's the matter?

Freddie Prinze Jr.: *(sniffling)* The way I treated you in that scene. I'm so sorry, Rachel.

Rachel Leigh Cook: *(laughing)* Don't be silly. It was just a scene.

Freddie Prinze Jr.: You don't understand. People treated me like that in high school. They treated me as if I was less than human. A piece of garbage. How was that okay with them? How did they sleep at night?

Narrator 2: Cook hugs him. Her eyes tear up.

Rachel Leigh Cook: You know what, Freddie? Those kids were all wrong. You were never a nerd. And you grew up to be a good man.

Scene 5

Narrator 1: Freddie goes on to star in many hit movies. But he stays away from the Hollywood nightlife. He doesn't want to repeat his father's mistakes. He never takes drugs. He doesn't drink. He spends his free time reading comic books and hanging out with friends.

Narrator 2: In 2002, Freddie marries actress Sarah Michelle Gellar. He tells reporters that he just wants to live "a normal life."

Narrator 1: It is a rainy day in Southern California. In a Los Angeles cemetery, Freddie walks up to a monument. Its plaque reads, "Freddie Prinze: 1955–1977." Freddie reaches out and touches the monument.

Freddie Prinze Jr.: Hey, Pop. I'm sorry that it took me so long to come out here, but I want to tell you something. After everything that's happened to me, I think I understand. The fame, the pressure . . . I know how hard it is. I think I know what you went through. And I want you to know that I'm here. I made it. And I hope you're proud of me.

Cross Outs

Freddie Prinze Jr.

	A	B	C
1	Freddie	*Boys and Girls*	*Summer Catch*
2	Prinze Jr.	reading comics	drugs
3	finds	hanging out	depression
4	super	strength	Sarah Michelle Geller

1. Cross out 2 things that led to Freddie Prinze's suicide in column C.

2. Cross out the names of 2 films in row 1.

3. Cross out two things Freddie Prinze Jr. likes to do in column B.

4. Cross out the name of the woman Freddie Prinze Jr. married in 2002.

Write the remaining words in order below.

_____ _____ _____ _____

_____.

Christopher Reeve

Actor and Spokesman

Summary

Christopher Reeve was an unknown actor when he landed the starring role in the 1978 film *Superman*. He went on to play the Man of Steel in three sequels. He also starred in seventeen movies, a dozen TV films, and more than 100 plays. His success allowed him to take up many hobbies. He was a pilot, a sailor, a scuba diver, a skier, and a horseman. In 1995, however, Reeve was thrown from his horse during a riding competition. Reeve broke his neck in the accident, and from that time, he was paralyzed from the neck down. Despite his injury, Reeve continued to work as an actor, director, author, and spokesman for people with spinal cord injuries until his death at age fifty-two on October 10, 2004.

Presentation Suggestions

Students can decorate the stage with movie posters representing the career of Christopher Reeve, including those of his four Superman movies. To emphasize the effects of Reeve's paralysis, the student reading Reeve's part can stand and move about before the accident, and sit in a wheelchair after the accident.

Related Books and Media

- Havil, Adrian. *Man of Steel: The Career and Courage of Christopher Reeve*. New York: Signet, 1996.

- Reeve, Christopher. *Still Me*. New York: Ballantine Books, 1999.

- Christopher Reeve Paralysis Foundation: www.apacure.com

Characters

Narrator 1

Narrator 2

Pierre Spengler, *producer of* Superman

Richard Donner, *director of* Superman

Christopher Reeve, *an actor*

Actress

Dana Reeve, *Christopher Reeve's wife*

Doctor

Reporter

Tom Welling, *star of the TV series* Smallville

Kristen Krueck, *Welling's costar*

Christopher Reeve
Actor and Spokesman

Scene 1

Narrator 1: The year is 1976. Two filmmakers, Richard Donner and Pierre Spengler, hold auditions for actors. They need someone to play a lead role in a blockbuster movie.

Pierre Spengler: This is a disaster. We start shooting in a month. We still haven't found our Superman yet. We should have picked a big star.

Richard Donner: I still think we need a fresh face. I don't want the audience to think he's just a big star wearing the costume.

Pierre Spengler: I know, I know. But we're running out of unknown actors to try out. We have one more left for today. What's his name?

Richard Donner: Reeve. Christopher Reeve.

Pierre Spengler *(calls across the soundstage)* Mr. Reeve? We're ready for you now.

Narrator 2: Christopher Reeve walks across the soundstage. He stands before the two men.

Reeve: Good to meet you.

Pierre Spengler: You too, Chris. We're just looking over your information. How old are you again?

Christopher Reeve: I'm twenty-four.

Pierre Spengler: *(to Donner)* He's too young. And too scrawny.

Richard Donner: *(to Spengler)* Give him a chance. *(to Reeve)* Okay, tell us how you would play Superman. How do you see the role?

Christopher Reeve: Well, I'd like to play him as someone with brains and a heart. I don't want just superpowers. What I think makes Superman a hero is that he uses his powers wisely.

Narrator 1: Spengler and Donner look at each other.

Pierre Spengler: Interesting . . .

Richard Donner: All right. Let's have you read a scene. This actress is going to read the role of reporter Lois Lane. She's invited you to her apartment for an interview. You've just landed on her balcony as the scene begins.

Narrator 2: Reeve takes a moment to prepare. He draws himself up and stands confidently. As he reads his first line, he seems to have changed from a young actor into a superhero.

Christopher Reeve: *(to the actress)* Good evening, Miss Lane.

Actress: Oh! I didn't see you there.

Christopher Reeve: I hope I didn't startle you.

Actress: No! I—it's just—well, not many people come to visit me by swooping out of the sky like that . . .

Christopher Reeve: I want to thank you for this interview. I'm sure people have a lot of questions about me.

Pierre Spengler: Wow . . .

Richard Donner: Pierre . . . I think we may have found our Superman.

Scene 2

Narrator 1: Reeve works for eighteen months on *Superman.* He builds up his body and performs many of his own stunts. He spends weeks harnessed to wires to film Superman's flying sequences.

Narrator 2: *Superman: The Movie* is released in 1978. It's a huge hit. Reeve becomes an international star. He stars in three *Superman* sequels, along with such films as *Deathtrap, Somewhere in Time,* and *The Remains of the Day.*

Narrator 1: Reeve also takes up a number of tough hobbies. He becomes a pilot. He flies across the Atlantic Ocean in a small plane twice. He also loves doing sports outdoors.

Narrator 2: In May 1995, Reeve competes in a horseback riding contest. His wife, Dana, is with him. They married in 1992.

Dana Reeve: How many events do you have left?

Christopher Reeve: Just the cross-country. It's got a few rail jumps. I think I can win it, though.

Dana Reeve: Be careful!

Christopher Reeve: I will, honey. See you at the finish line!

Narrator 1: Reeve speeds through the course. Soon, he and his horse approach a rail jump. Reeve can tell the horse is nervous.

Christopher Reeve: Come on, buddy. You can do it. You can—

Narrator 2: Suddenly, the horse skids to a halt. Reeve is thrown in the air. He lands headfirst with a sickening thud.

Dana Reeve: Oh, no! Chris!

Narrator 1: Reeve lies motionless. A crowd rushes to his side.

Dana Reeve: Nobody touch him! Don't move him! He could have injured his neck! Chris, stay still. There's an ambulance on the way.

Narrator 2: Reeve is taken to a nearby hospital. Dana waits nervously for news. After several hours, a doctor comes to see her.

Dana Reeve: How is he?

Doctor: Mrs. Reeve, your husband has fractured two vertebrae in his neck. We're going to have to fuse them together. We literally need to re-attach his head to his spinal column.

Dana Reeve: Oh, no . . .

Doctor: There's also been severe damage to his spinal cord. Your husband is paralyzed from the neck down. He can't breathe without the help of a machine. And he'll never walk again.

Dana Reeve: Oh, no. Chris . . . poor Chris . . .

Doctor: He's awake now. You can go see him.

Scene 3

Narrator 1: Reeve lies in bed in a hospital room. He's hooked up to several machines. One of them breathes for him through a tube in his neck. The others keep track of his vital signs.

Narrator 2: Reeve stares at the ceiling. Dana enters the room. She steps to the side of his bed.

Dana Reeve: Chris? Chris, can you hear me?

Narrator 1: She takes his hand in hers. Reeve has trouble speaking. Still, he manages to get the words out.

Christopher Reeve: Are you . . . holding my hand?

Dana Reeve: Yes.

Christopher Reeve: I . . . I can't feel it.

Narrator 2: The two say nothing for a few moments. The only sound in the room is the machine that pushes air into Reeve's lungs.

Christopher Reeve: Dana . . . I've been thinking. Maybe . . . maybe we should . . . let me go.

Dana Reeve: What?

Christopher Reeve: Maybe we should . . . tell the doctors . . . to unhook the machines. Let me go.

Dana Reeve: *(in tears)* Listen to me, Chris. I'm only going to say this once. I'll support whatever you want to do, because it's your life. But I want you to know that I'll be with you for the long haul. No matter what.

Narrator 1: Reeve's eyes turn to the side, and he makes eye contact with his wife.

Dana Reeve: You're still you. And I love you.

Narrator 2: The two look at each other. They don't say anything more.

Scene 4

Narrator 1: Eventually, Reeve is released from the hospital. He spends six months at a medical center. He learns to drive a special electric wheelchair. He makes it move by sipping or puffing on a straw. A machine measures the sips and puffs and makes the wheelchair move.

Narrator 2: In 1998, he writes the story of his life. He remembers Dana's words. He thinks those words that she said saved his life. He titles the book *Still Me*.

Narrator 1: Several years later, a reporter visits Reeve at his home.

Reporter: Chris, since your injury, you've directed and starred in TV movies. You've traveled around the country to speak about spinal cord injuries and research. You've done all this from your wheelchair. How do you do it?

Christopher Reeve: I have to do it. Acting and directing are what I do. And there have been many advances in the search for a cure for spinal cord injuries. Someday, doctors will reconnect my nerves. After that, I'm going to stand up. I will thank all the people who have helped me through this.

Reporter: How do you feel?

Christopher Reeve: Since the accident, I've had a lot of physical problems. But there have also been days when I've felt great. I miss freedom and adventure more than I can say. But I love my family. I love my work. And someday, I will walk again.

Narrator 2: Dana enters.

Dana Reeve: Chris, it's almost time to go.

Christopher Reeve: Thanks, honey.

Reporter: Where are you off to next?

Christopher Reeve: I'm doing a guest shot on a TV show. *(He smiles)* Just a small role.

Scene 5

Narrator 1: It is January 2003 on the set of the TV show *Smallville*. The show tells the story of a modern-day, teenaged Clark Kent. In the show, young Clark adjusts to the superpowers that he will someday use as Superman.

Narrator 2: On the set are Tom Welling, the actor who plays Clark, and Kristen Kruek, who plays his friend, Lana Lang. They wait nervously for their special guest star to arrive.

Tom Welling: This is going to be so cool.

Kristen Kruek: So he's playing the scientist who tells Clark the truth about who he is and where he came from?

Tom Welling: Yeah. This is a big episode. And I can't wait to meet him.

Narrator 1: Suddenly, the crew bursts into applause. Reeve rolls onto the set in his wheelchair. Dana is at his side.

Kristen Kruek: Wow. There he is!

Narrator 2: Welling takes a deep breath. He and Kruek walk across the set to Reeve.

Tom Welling: Mr. Reeve? Hi. I'm Tom Welling. It's great to finally meet you.

Christopher Reeve: It's nice to meet you, too. How old are you, Tom?

Tom Welling: Actually, I'm twenty-five. I know, I'm a little old to be playing someone in high school.

Christopher Reeve: *(smiling)* It's okay. As long as you have the brains and a good heart, I think Superman will be fine.

Christopher Reeve

	A	**B**	**C**
1	Lois Lane	determination	pilot
2	brains	is	heart
3	a	super	spinal cord
4	Smallville	power	outdoorsman

1. Cross out the two things Christopher Reeve becomes after *Superman* in column C.

2. Cross out the body part Reeve injures in row 3.

3. Cross out the things that Reeve says are most important to Superman in row 2.

4. Cross out the name of a character from the movie *Superman* in row 1.

5. Cross out the name of the town in which Clark Kent grows up in column A.

Write the remaining words in order below.

_____ _____ _____ _____

_____ .

Franklin Delano Roosevelt

President

Summary

Franklin Delano Roosevelt was born in wealth and privilege to an upper-class family in Hyde Park, New York. As a child, he seemed destined to live his life as a gentleman socialite, living off the family name and fortune. Instead, Roosevelt grew up to become not only the thirty-second president of the United States, but also a champion of the common man. Leading the country through the Great Depression of the 1930s, Roosevelt symbolized hope, strength, and eternal optimism in one of America's darkest periods. Later, as World War II ravaged the globe, FDR again proved his leadership, guiding an American effort that beat back tyranny around the world.

But perhaps the most amazing part of the Roosevelt story is that he fulfilled his destiny from the confines of a wheelchair. After suffering a polio attack in 1921 at the age of thirty-nine, FDR became paralyzed from the waist down. Publicly, he never let his disability interfere with his duties. In fact, he rarely acknowledged his disability in public at all. Instead of allowing his disability to define him, Roosevelt forged a legacy that consistently ranks him by scholars and historians as one of the greatest of American presidents.

Presentation Suggestions

Before reading the play, students might get a feel for the period of Roosevelt's presidency by decorating the room with pictures and posters from the Great Depression and World War II. Students could also get a sense of the challenges Roosevelt faced by sitting in a wheelchair and moving around the classroom and their school.

Related Books and Media

- Bardhan-Quallen, Sudipta. *Franklin Delano Roosevelt: A National Hero (Sterling Biographies)*. New York, NY: Sterling Publishing Co., Inc. 2007.

- Thompson, Gare. *Who Was Eleanor Roosevelt?* New York, NY: Grosset & Dunlap, 2004.

- The Franklin D. Roosevelt Presidential Library and Museum: http://www.fdrlibrary.marist.edu/

Characters

Tour Guide 1	Anna Roosevelt, *FDR's daughter*
Tour Guide 2	Eleanor Roosevelt, *FDR's wife*
James Roosevelt, *FDR's father*	Elliot Roosevelt, *FDR's son*
Franklin D. Roosevelt	Winston Churchill, *prime minister of Great Britain*
Sarah Roosevelt, *FDR's mother*	Artist

Franklin Delano Roosevelt President

Scene 1

Tour Guide 1: Good morning, everyone. Welcome to Hyde Park, New York. This is where Franklin Delano Roosevelt, the thirty-second president of the United States, was born. And this is where he was laid to rest.

Tour Guide 2: Most historians agree that three presidents tower over U.S. history. One was George Washington. He is often called "the father of our country." The second was Abraham Lincoln. He preserved the nation during the Civil War. And the third was Franklin Roosevelt. He led the country during its most troubled times of the twentieth century.

Tour Guide 1: But Roosevelt was chosen to lead his people despite the fact that he couldn't stand or walk without help.

Tour Guide 2: Roosevelt is often referred to by his initials, FDR. He was born to a wealthy family here in Hyde Park. His family traveled often. They spent many summers at their home on Campobello Island in New Brunswick, Canada.

Tour Guide 1: An accident he suffered there as a boy would give an early hint of the man he would become. Roosevelt was hiking in the woods with his father and mother . . .

Scene 2

James Roosevelt: Come, Franklin! You and Mother must keep up if we're to make it back in time for dinner!

Franklin D. Roosevelt: I'm coming, Father!

Sarah Roosevelt: Now, I want you to be careful, Franklin.

James Roosevelt: Don't baby him, Sarah. The boy has to learn how to be tough!

FDR: Don't slow down the pace for me, Father!

Sarah Roosevelt: Franklin, be careful on that rock ledge. It looks slippery!

FDR: Nonsense! I can make it! I can—whoa!

Sarah Roosevelt: Franklin!

Tour Guide 2: The boy fell from the ledge. He struck his mouth against a tree branch on the way down. His parents rushed to his side.

FDR: Ooohh!

Sarah Roosevelt: Oh, no! Is he all right?

James Roosevelt: He seems to have broken a few teeth.

FDR: Father! Father, it hurts!

James Roosevelt: I know, son. I know. We'll get you to a doctor as soon as we can. But we're in the middle of the wilderness. You're going to have to bear the pain without fuss until we get there. Can you do it?

FDR: I . . . I . . . yes, Father. I can do it.

James Roosevelt: Good man. Let's go, then. On your feet. Gently . . .

Scene 3

Tour Guide 1: FDR grew up and went into politics. He became a state senator. Later, he served as assistant secretary of the Navy. He married, and he and his wife Eleanor had children of their own.

Tour Guide 2: It was back at Campobello Island, during a family vacation in 1921, that FDR's life would change forever.

Anna Roosevelt: Father, come play with us!

FDR: Anna, isn't it your bedtime?

Anna Roosevelt:	No, not for another two hours. Come and play!
FDR:	Not now, sweetheart.
Eleanor Roosevelt:	Franklin, are you all right?
FDR:	I don't know. I'm exhausted. And I have a pain in my leg that won't go away.
Anna Roosevelt:	Father, please!
Eleanor Roosevelt:	Anna, leave your father alone. Franklin, maybe you should go lie down.
FDR:	Yes. Perhaps you're right. I think I'll go to bed early . . .
Tour Guide 1:	By the next morning, his condition was worse.
FDR:	My legs, Eleanor . . . they're so weak. I can't stand. I don't know what's the matter with me . . .
Eleanor Roosevelt:	You're running a fever, Franklin. It's 102. We have to get you to a doctor right away.
FDR:	All right. But please . . . don't tell my mother. Since Father passed away, she worries about me so. And I don't want to frighten the children. Let's . . . let's not make a fuss.

Scene 4

Tour Guide 2:	The doctor confirmed the Roosevelts' worst fears. FDR had polio. It's a disease that causes muscles to become paralyzed.
Tour Guide 1:	Today, polio has been all but wiped out. But in 1921, there was an outbreak of the disease. It terrified the public.
Tour Guide 2:	Roosevelt's attack left him paralyzed for life from the waist down.
Tour Guide 1:	Eventually, though, FDR resumed his political career. He used a wheelchair to get around when he was alone. He sometimes wore a heavy set of iron

braces on his legs. When he wore the braces, he could lean on someone's arm and appear to walk. And he could hold onto a podium to stand up and deliver speeches.

FDR: Ladies and gentlemen . . . I will run for president of the United States!

Tour Guide 2: In 1931, the country was in the midst of the Great Depression. One quarter of the American people were out of work. Two million were homeless. FDR faced the depression bravely.

FDR: My fellow citizens, I pledge you, I pledge myself, to a new deal for the American people!

Tour Guide 1: FDR won in a landslide. On election night, FDR's son took off his father's braces and helped him into bed.

Elliot Roosevelt: You did it, Dad. You did it!

FDR: *We* did it, son.

Elliot Roosevelt: Well, what's the matter? Aren't you happy?

FDR: Of course. But . . .

Elliot Roosevelt: But what?

FDR: I'll let you in on a secret, son. All my life, I've only been afraid of one thing: fire. Tonight, I think I'm afraid of something else.

Elliot Roosevelt: What's that, Dad?

FDR: I'm afraid I may not have the strength to do this job.

Elliot Roosevelt: Don't worry, Dad. You're the strongest man I know.

FDR: Thank you, son. You know, son. Maybe there's only one thing any of us needs to be afraid of . . . .

Scene 5

Tour Guide 2: Soon, FDR was sworn in as America's thirty-second president. He set out to restore the American people's faith in their country—and themselves.

FDR: First of all, let me assert my firm belief that the only thing we have to fear is—fear itself!

Tour Guide 1: FDR and the Congress passed a flurry of bills to help the country. America began to regain confidence in itself.

Tour Guide 2: All the while, FDR never drew attention to his condition. The people knew that their president was disabled—but it didn't change their opinion of him.

Scene 6

Tour Guide 1: FDR was reelected in 1936. In 1940, he became the first president to win a third term to the White House.

Tour Guide 2: By then, though, war was brewing in Europe and in Asia. Soon, the United States was drawn into the war. Then the unthinkable happened.

FDR: Yesterday, December 7, 1941—a date which will live in infamy—the United States of America was suddenly and deliberately attacked by the naval and air forces of the empire of Japan . . .

Tour Guide 1: FDR threw himself into winning the war. World leaders like Winston Churchill, prime minister of England, admired him.

Winston Churchill: The president has scored a great triumph over his disability. Perhaps he is an example of a man who has had his physical strength taken away, but who, at the same time, has gained a tremendous strength of character.

Tour Guide 2: FDR continued to inspire the country.

FDR: We are united in seeking the kind of victory that will guarantee that our grandchildren may grow and live their lives free of the constant threat of invasion, destruction, and slavery!

Scene 7

Tour Guide 1: In 1944, FDR was elected to a historic fourth term.

Tour Guide 2: By 1945, victory in World War II was within sight. By now, FDR's appearance was showing how hard it was to be president. His health had grown much worse.

Tour Guide 1: On April 12, 1945, FDR was visiting his vacation retreat in Warm Springs, Georgia. He was having his portrait painted.

FDR: How much longer will this be?

Artist: I'm almost done for today, Mr. President. Are you feeling all right? Forgive me for saying so, but you're not looking well.

FDR: I have a terrific headache . . . *(he slumps over on his desk)*

Artist: Mr. President? Mr. President!

Scene 8

Tour Guide 2: FDR's death shocked the United States, and the world.

Winston Churchill: President Roosevelt's disability lay heavily upon him. It was a marvel that he bore up against it. Not one man in ten million, stricken as he was, would have attempted to live the life he led. Not one in ten million would have tried. Not one in a generation could have succeeded. His was a story of spirit over the flesh, of willpower over physical ailment.

He brought his country through the worst of its perils. He saw it through the greatest of its toils. He is the greatest champion of freedom who has ever brought help and comfort from his shores to ours.

Tour Guide 1: Today, decades after his death, FDR, his life, and his words continue to inspire Americans.

FDR: The only limit to our realization of tomorrow will be our doubts of today. Let us move forward with strong, active faith.

Franklin D. Roosevelt

	A	B	C
1	disease	great	New York
2	president	war	strength
3	wheelchair	comes	library
4	from	muscles	within

1. Cross out the word for illness in row 1.

2. Cross out the name of FDR's home state in column C.

3. Cross out the word for the leader of the United States in row 2.

4. Cross out the word for the opposite of peace in column B.

5. Cross out the name of a device used by disabled people in column A.

6. Cross out the word for where books are kept in column C.

7. Cross out the word for part of the human body in row 4.

Write the remaining words in order below.

_____ _____ _____ _____

_____.

Erik Weihenmayer

Blind Mountain Climber

Summary

Erik Weihenmayer was diagnosed with retinoschisis, a rare eye disease, when he was a young child. By the time he was in high school, he was totally blind. Thanks to loving parents, a variety of experiences in remote places around the world, and strong athletic ability, Erik has set and met a variety of challenges. His greatest achievement, climbing Mt. Everest, was achieved in May 2002.

Presentation Suggestions

Much of the play takes place in school settings. A mural showing various mountain peaks could be displayed. Students can be encouraged to find books about Mt. Everest or other famous mountains, such as Mt. Kilimanjaro.

Related Book and Media

- Weihenmayer, Erik. *Touch the Top of the World*. New York: Penguin Putnam, 2002.
- Erik Weihenmayer: www.touchthetop.com

Characters

Narrator 1	Erik Weihenmayer
Narrator 2	Mrs. Mundy, *Erik's teacher*
Mom	Mark, *Erik's brother*
Dad	Eddi, *Erik's brother*
Doctor	Ellen, *Erik's wife*
Principal	

Erik Weihenmayer Blind Mountain Climber

Scene 1

Narrator 1: Erik is a just a baby when his dad notices his eyes shake a lot. He has Erik's mom look at them. She sees the same problem. She tries not to worry.

Mom: There's probably nothing wrong.

Dad: I think we should take him to a doctor.

Mom: I'll call. But I bet it's nothing.

Narrator 2: But there is something wrong. Erik can't see well. No one is quite sure what is wrong. Erik's parents take him to lots of doctors.

Narrator 1: For two years they ask questions. One famous doctor figures out what is wrong. Then he gives them the bad news.

Doctor: Erik has a rare eye disease. He can't see things that are straight ahead.

Mom: Can he see at all?

Doctor: He can see a bit to the sides.

Mom: So he'll be able to get around.

Doctor: He'll be able to get around for a few years.

Mom: We can get him glasses, too. Right?

Doctor: Glasses will help for a while. But we can't stop the damage. Then he'll be totally blind.

Dad: How much time before he's blind?

Doctor: We don't know for sure.

Dad: You have to have some idea.

Doctor: He will be blind by his early teens. I'm sorry.

Narrator 2: Erik's parents give Erik lots of help. He wears thick glasses. He can see letters a little.

Narrator 1: Soon it's time for him to go to kindergarten. His mother takes him to a good school. She meets with the principal.

Principal: I'm afraid that Erik would have a hard time at our school. I don't think he would do well here.

Mom: I know he can't see well. But I will help him.

Principal: I know you'd help. But he would do better at a school for the blind. They could teach him things we can't teach.

Mom: Like what? Tuning pianos? That's what most blind people do. There is nothing wrong with tuning pianos. But my son needs to learn many things. He is going to the top. Just you watch.

Principal: How will he manage the school work?

Mom: He's smart. He'll work hard.

Principal: We don't have the extra staff to help him.

Mom: I'll help him. I'll come to class and work with him.

Principal: Let me think about it. I'll let you know.

Narrator 2: The principal lets Erik attend the school with his mother's help.

Scene 2

Narrator 1: Erik's father's job takes the family to Hong Kong. They enjoy the adventure. Erik and his brother explore Hong Kong together.

Narrator 2: After four years they move back to the United States. By now, Erik is slowly going blind. He tries to deal with it. But he's angry much of the time.

Narrator 1: Erik is totally blind by the time he starts high school. His mom drives him on the first day.

Mom: Let me walk you inside.

Erik Weihenmayer: No. I want to do this by myself.

Narrator 2: Erik has just begun using a cane. He wants to do things his own way. But he doesn't usc the cane well. He fumbles his way into the school.

Narrator 1: Mrs. Mundy is a teacher for the blind. She meets with Erik.

Mrs. Mundy: Hello, Erik. I'll be helping you at school. The first thing you need to do is learn how to use that cane right.

Erik Weihenmayer: I don't need your help.

Mrs. Mundy: You can learn to use it the right way. Or I can take you to all your classes. What's it going to be?

Erik Weihenmayer: All right. Take me to class for now.

Mrs. Mundy: Let's go. You'll have textbooks in Braille. You'll be able to follow along.

Narrator 2: Erik struggles to keep up with the teachers. He realizes after a while that he doesn't know where the bathroom is. He leaves class, hoping to find it. He doesn't want to ask for help.

Narrator 1: Mrs. Mundy finds him alone in the hall. He hasn't found the bathroom.

Mrs. Mundy: What are you doing out here? Take my arm. I'll take you back to class.

Erik Weihenmayer: I can't go back to class.

Mrs. Mundy: You can and you will.

Erik Weihenmayer: No, I won't.

Mrs. Mundy: Yes, you will.

Erik Weihenmayer: *(quietly)* I won't. I couldn't find the bathroom. I just peed in my pants. I haven't done that since I was a little kid. I won't go back today.

Narrator 2: Mrs. Mundy sees that Erik gets home. The next day they get to work. Erik learns how to get by. He makes friends with another student. That winter he decides to try out for the wrestling team.

Narrator 1: Erik finds he is a good wrestler. The next summer he goes to a wrestling camp. One day he gets called to the office. His father is there.

Dad: Erik. I'm so sorry, son. Your mother was in a car accident. She was killed.

Erik Weihenmayer: No! That can't be right.

Dad: I'm sorry, Erik.

Narrator 2: Erik struggles through the rest of the summer. He misses his mother terribly. She had always believed in him.

Narrator 1: Erik starts his sophomore year at high school. He wonders if he'll ever get over losing the person who believed in him the most.

Scene 3

Narrator 2: During the next few years Erik adjusts to life without his mother. His brothers are at college. He and his dad live alone.

Narrator 1: Eric has one bright spot. He gets a guide dog and names him Wizard. He and Wizard become best friends.

Narrator 2: Erik also learns rock climbing. He continues wrestling. He goes to college too. Then he has another setback. His left eye starts to hurt. He goes to see the eye doctor again.

Doctor: Erik, there is a lot of pressure in your eye. The best choice is to have it removed.

Erik Weihenmayer: Then what? I'll just have a hole?

Doctor: You can have an eye made after you have healed.

Erik Weihenmayer: A glass eye?

Doctor: It is made of plastic. It will be painted to look very real.

Narrator 1: Erik has the surgery. He returns to finish his first year at college. That summer his dad decides that Erik and his brothers should do something together.

Dad: What do you think, fellows? How about a family trip?

Erik Weihenmayer: How about a hiking trip?

Mark: That sounds great, Erik. Where?

Erik Weihenmayer: How about Peru? I have a flyer about it. There's a great place called the Inca Trail.

Eddi: Let me see that.. . . This says it takes seven days. Do you think they'll let you hike it, Erik?

Erik Weihenmayer: I'll talk to them.

Eddi: Then I'm in.

Mark: I'm not going to miss out.

Dad: I'll call them. This could be great.

Narrator 2: No blind person has ever hiked the Inca Trail. However, Erik is a good athlete. The people in charge let him hike the trail. The hike is a big success.

Narrator 1: The family decides to visit many remote areas of the world. Each trip gives Erik more confidence. On one trip, Mark helps guide Erik.

Erik Weihenmayer: Mark, is it hard to guide me?

Mark: I could do this any time. Guiding you is easy.

Erik Weihenmayer: Thanks, Mark. I know it can't be that much fun helping out a blind man.

Mark: Erik, don't think about that. If I could give you one of my eyes, I would. I wish I could help more.

Narrator 2: Erik graduates from college. He gets a job teaching fifth graders. At first it's hard to teach. He learns how to use the students to help. They learn together.

Narrator 1: He also learns to like Ellen, another teacher. One day they are having coffee together.

Ellen: Erik, when are you getting married?

Erik Weihenmayer: *What?*

Ellen: Aren't you engaged?

Erik Weihenmayer: Well . . . I told the principal I was. I wanted to teach so much. I thought being engaged might help.

Ellen: *(laughing)* Are you serious?

Erik Weihenmayer: I'm afraid so.

Ellen: Well, I'm glad you're not engaged.

Narrator 2: Erik and Ellen begin seeing each other a lot. They try to keep their romance a secret. However, one day Wizard is supposed to take Erik to an empty chair in a teachers' meeting. Instead he goes right to Ellen's chair. He puts his head in her lap. All the other teachers laugh.

Narrator 1: The secret is out. Erik and Ellen get married on Mount Kilimanjaro on a plateau 13,000 feet high. Erik feels like he is on top of the world.

Epilogue

Narrator 2: Erik loves to climb. He climbs many famous mountain peaks around the world. He is on radio and television shows. He talks about reaching goals.

Narrator 1: Erik's greatest climb comes in May 2001. He and other talented climbers climb to the top of Mount Everest. It is the tallest mountain in the world. Many people have died trying to climb it.

Narrator 2: Eric thinks about his mother a lot. Just as she said, he has proven that a blind man can do anything. He can even climb to the top of the world.

# Cross Outs

Erik Weihenmayer

	A	B	C
1	reach	Hong Kong	the
2	eye	cane	heights
3	Wizard	of	Kilimanjaro
4	success	Braille	Everest

1. Cross out the city where Erik once lived as a child in row 1.

2. Cross out the kind of disease Erik has in column A.

3. Cross out the things that help Erik read and get around in column B.

4. Cross out the name of Erik's dog in row 3.

5. Cross out the names of two mountains that Erik climbs in column C.

Write the remaining words in order below.

_____ _____ _____ _____

_____.

Bob Woodruff

News Correspondent

Summary

Bob Woodruff was a news anchor for *World News Tonight* on ABC. On January 29, 2006, while on assignment near Taji, Iraq, he and Canadian cameraman Doug Vogt were standing with their heads above a hatch in a Humvee. Enemy insurgents launched an IED (improvised explosive device), and both men were seriously injured. After initial treatment at a military hospital, the men were flown to Germany for further treatment. Part of Woodruff's skull was removed to allow for his brain's swelling. Upon his return home, Woodruff faced more surgery and nearly a year of rehabilitation.

Presentation Suggestions

A map of the Middle East, military paraphernalia, or photographs of Iraq can be placed on stage. Bob Woodruff can sit in a chair during the presentation. The ABC news anchors sit at a desk. Other readers can stand or sit on stools.

Related Book and Media

- Woodruff, Lee, and Bob Woodruff. *In an Instant: A Family's Journey of Love and Healing.* New York: Random House, 2007.

- http://www.bobwoodrufffamilyfund.org/

Characters

Narrator 1

Narrator 2

Bob Woodruff, *ABC News Anchor*

Doug Vogt, *ABC Cameraman*

Vinne Malhotra, *ABC Producer*

Driver

Magnus Macedo, *ABC Soundman*

Soldier

Kate Snow, *ABC Reporter*

Bill Weir, *ABC Reporter*

David Westin, *ABC President*

Lee Woodruff, *Bob Woodruff's wife*

Doctor 1

Doctor 2

David Woodruff, *Bob Woodruff's brother*

Doctor 3

Bob Woodruff
News Correspondent

Scene 1

Narrator 1: An ABC news team stands by a Humvee. They are at a camp in Iraq. They are doing a story on the war. It is January 2006.

Bob Woodruff: What a great trip so far! We have talked to lots of soldiers.

Doug Vogt: And I have gotten some great pictures.

Vinnie Malhotra: I hope we learn more at the water treatment plant. This will be a big story!

Driver: Let's get going. Get below, everyone.

Doug Vogt: I want to stand up so I can shoot some film.

Bob Woodruff: I want to stand too. I want to report on what we see.

Driver: Okay. But be careful. There is more risk up there. Magnus? What about you?

Magnus Macedo: First, I need to fix some sound gear. The tank may be too loud to hear you, Bob. Then I'll come up.

Driver: Let's get on our way. Watch for signs of a bomb. You never know what has been put in the road.

Narrator 1: The team drives a few miles. Doug and Bob are standing up in the tank. There is a huge blast. Rocks fly through the air. They don't know what hit them.

Vinnie Malhotra: Magnus! Help me! Bob and Doug have been hit!

Narrator 2: Doug is hit in head. But his helmet stays on. Bob isn't so lucky. He is hit by lots of big and small rocks. His helmet flies off. Blood pours out of a hole in his neck.

Magnus Macedo: Hang on Bob! You're going to be okay! We are going to get you out of here. Hang on, Doug!

Vinnie Malhotra: Medic! We need help! Medic!

Soldier: There are no medics. Just hang on. We'll get you out of here.

Bob Woodruff: What happened? This hurts! Why is there so much blood?

Soldier: Hang on. Hang on . . .

Scene 2

Narrator 2: New York City is far away from Iraq. It is a cold Sunday morning there. An ABC team is reading the news on TV.

Kate Snow: We have a new report, Bill. We just got word of an attack in Iraq. An ABC news team is there. They were in a tank. A bomb went off.

Bill Weir: What do we know about the team? Are they okay?

Kate Snow: The blast was very strong. Some of the team is fine. But some were hurt. They are on the way to the hospital. We are waiting for more news.

Bill Weir: Let's keep the team in our thoughts. We will be back with more news.

Scene 3

Narrator 1: Bob's wife is asleep in a hotel room. Lee and the kids are at Disney World for the weekend. The phone rings. Lee thinks it's a wake-up call. It's not. It's the president of ABC News.

Lee Woodruff: Thank you. I'm awake.

Narrator 2: Lee starts to hang up the phone.

David Westin: Lee? It's David Westin.

Lee Woodruff: What is it?

David Westin: Lee, Bob has been hurt. We don't know how bad it is. We are getting help for him.

Lee Woodruff: Is he alive?

David Westin: Yes. But his head was hurt in the blast.

Lee Woodruff: Oh no! Tell me what happened.

Narrator 1: David tells Lee what he knows. Then he tells her that a plane is waiting for her. Lee hangs up and starts calling her family. Then she leaves for the airport.

Narrator 2: Bob is in surgery while Lee is on the plane. Her cell phone rings. It is the doctor.

Doctor 1: The blast hit Bob's skull. We had to remove a lot of bone. We don't know how his brain is. We don't know if his left eye and ear will be okay. We must take him to Germany as soon as we can.

Lee Woodruff: He's alive? Will he live?

Doctor 1: He is alive.

Scene 4

Narrator 1: Military doctors treat Bob first. He gets very good care. Doug is not hurt as much as Bob. Both men are sent to Germany as soon as it is safe.

Narrator 2: Lee talks to the doctor when she gets there. Bob's brother, David, is with her.

Doctor 2: Bob's brain will swell from the blast. So we had to remove half of his skull. We also had to take out a lot of rocks from his body.

David Woodruff: Will he be okay?

Doctor 2: It will take a long time. It could take one or two years.

David Woodruff: Can we see him?

Doctor 2: Yes. He is in a coma. But you can talk to him. Don't stay long.

Narrator 1: Bob's head is partly shaved. One side looks okay. The other side is badly swollen. Tubes go from his body to machines.

Narrator 2: Lee and David talk to Bob for a while. He seems sound asleep. He looks terrible. But Lee knows that he is still Bob. She knows he will get better.

Scene 5

Narrator 1: A few days pass. Bob and Doug go back to the United States. They fly in a special plane. A team of doctors and nurses goes with them.

Narrator 2: Lee's friends and family take care of the kids. Lee stays with Bob. A month later, the doctors remove a big rock. Bob gets very sick. At last, Bob wakes up. It is three weeks after the blast. Lee talks to him.

Lee Woodruff: Bob, you were in a blast. You are going to be fine, Bob. I am here.

Narrator 1: Bob acts like he wants to talk.

Lee Woodruff: You can't talk. There's a tube in your throat. Just rest, Bob.

Narrator 2: Bob starts to get better. He still sleeps most of the time. The doctor warns Lee that Bob needs a lot of time.

Doctor 2: We don't know how Bob will change.

Lee Woodruff: What do you mean?

Doctor 2: He may not be able to think right. He may have a hard time thinking of a word.

Lee Woodruff: What else?

Doctor 2: He may be sad. He may forget normal things like how to get dressed. He may not seem like the man you know.

Lee Woodruff: Will he be able to do his job?

Doctor 2: He may have to work less. It is hard to know.

Scene 6

Narrator 1: Bob stays asleep most of the time. At last, he really wakes up. It has been thirty-six days. He does not know where he is. Lee tells him about the blast.

Bob Woodruff: I don't remember much. Who else was hurt?

Lee Woodruff: Doug was hurt. He is much better. He went home. How do you feel?

Bob Woodruff: I hurt. I hurt a lot. But, Lee. How are the kids?

Lee Woodruff: They are fine. Let's call them.

Narrator 2: Bob finds that his body gets better fast. His brain is slower. He can't think of some words. He can't write. He is sad that he got hurt. He feels sorry for his family. A doctor meets with Lee. She learns about Bob's tests.

Doctor 3: Bob's brain is not doing well yet.

Lee Woodruff: What do you mean?

Doctor 3: He has poor memory. His language skills are poor.

Lee Woodruff: Will he get better?

Doctor 3: I think he will. He just starting to heal. He has a long way to go. But you will see him getting better every day.

Lee Woodruff: Can I take him home?

Doctor 3: That is a good idea. He can get rehab close to home.

Scene 7

Narrator 1: Bob works hard at getting better. He remembers many words. But he forgets simple words. Every day he learns more. He practices words by doing things like looking at plastic fruits.

Bob Woodruff: Apple . . . banana . . . orange.. . . Wait. I know what that one is. I just can't say it.

Lee Woodruff: Take your time. You'll think of it.

Bob Woodruff: Pear . . . no . . . peach!

Lee Woodruff: Great!

Narrator 2: Bob has to have an operation too. His head needs a new skull plate so it will look normal. Bob loves the way his head feels now.

Bob Woodruff: Lee, feel my head! It's round! And I don't get dizzy when I move it.

Lee Woodruff: You look great, Bob!

Narrator 1: It has been four months since Bob was hurt. He and Doug were lucky they lived. Two members of a CBS news team are not so lucky. A car bomb hits their team. Two people die. One reporter clings to life. Like Bob and Doug, she makes it.

Narrator 2: A year passes. Bob goes back to work. He still does what he knows best. He reports the news.

Cross Outs

Bob Woodruff

	A	B	C
1	brain	news	reporter
2	Bob	Iraq	doesn't
3	let	a	rocks
4	blast	stop	him

1. Cross out the part of Bob that gets hurt the most in column A.

2. Cross out the country in which Bob is hurt in column B.

3. Cross out what doctors take out of Bob's body in column C.

4. Cross out the two words that tell Bob's job in row 1.

Write the remaining words in order below.

_____ _____ _____ _____

_____ _____ _____ .

Special Guests

Jewel (Singer/Songwriter), Jay Leno (Talk Show Host), Nancy Cartwright (Bart Simpson's Voice), and Bob Dole (Senator)

Summary

In this script, a group of famous people visit a school. The visitors include Jewel, singer/songwriter; Jay Leno, comedian and talk show host; Nancy Cartwright, the voice of TV's Bart Simpson; and Bob Dole, former senator and presidential candidate. The school guests talk about the challenges they overcame on their way to success. This script can be used as a model for students as they write their own scripts about people who have overcome difficulties in their lives.

Presentation Suggestions

Each narrator is paired with a guest. The script can then be read as if an interview is taking place. Students can sit beside their interview subjects in a conversational setting.

Related Media

- List of biographies and autobiographies about people who beat the odds: http://sachem.suffolk.lib.ny.us/advisor/bioadversity.htm.

- List of famous people with disabilities: http://www.disabled-world.com

Characters

Teacher

Student 1

Jewel, *singer*

Student 2

Jay Leno, *TV celebrity*

Student 3

Nancy Cartwright, *voice of Bart Simpson*

Student 4

Bob Dole, *U.S. Senator*

 **Special Guests**

Scene 1

Teacher: Hello, students. Today, four special guests are visiting us. They have all overcome tough times. They have all risen to the top of their fields. And today, students from our school will interview them. Our first guest is one of today's most popular singers and songwriters. Please welcome Jewel.

Student 1: Hi, Jewel. Thanks for coming today.

Jewel: Thank you. It's great to be here.

Student 1: You had an unusual childhood. Tell us about how you grew up.

Jewel: I grew up on an 800-acre homestead in Homer, Alaska. We were way out in the middle of nowhere. There was no shower, no TV—not even a bathroom! We had to use an outhouse. It was usually pretty cold!

Student 1: Your family was very musical, weren't they?

Jewel: Yes. We used to put on family talent shows to entertain each other. Music was important to me. So was writing. My parents got divorced when I was just a kid. I kept a journal about my thoughts and feelings. It was really helpful.

Student 1: What was your formal training in music?

Jewel: I finished high school at the Interlochen Fine Arts Academy in Michigan. I studied opera there. After that, I moved to San Diego, California. I tried working a few jobs, like waiting tables and stuff like that. But they never worked out. I wasn't happy. I wanted to work on my music.

Student 1: What did you do?

Jewel: I was broke. So I moved out of my apartment. I lived in a van. I spent as much time as I could writing music. I also began playing at local clubs and cafes. That helped me bring in a little bit of money.

Student 1: Then what happened?

Jewel: I began to develop a following. Some record executives came to see me play. They offered me a record contract.

Student 1: Your first album, *Pieces of You,* sold 11 million copies, didn't it?

Jewel: Yes, it did. I've done several other albums since then. I've also written a book of poetry.

Student 1: You've worked so hard. I wish we had more time. Thanks again for visiting us.

Jewel: My pleasure!

Scene 2

Teacher: Our next visitor also comes from the world of show business. Let's welcome comedian Jay Leno.

Student 2: Hi, Jay. Tell us about your TV show.

Jay Leno: I'm the host of *The Tonight Show*. It's on late at night. A lot of you kids might not have seen it. But the show has been on since 1954. I took over after the last host retired. His name was Johnny Carson. For years, he was the king of late-night TV. I was really honored to get the job.

Student 2: How did you get into show business?

Jay Leno: When I was a kid, I wasn't a very good student. I had the attention span of a flea. I still do. But as a kid, I made people laugh. I was the class clown.

Student 2: So you wanted to be a comedian since you were a kid?

Jay Leno: Not really. I had no idea what I was going to do. My father was a salesman. I just thought I'd be a funny salesman. But when I went to college, I started performing in comedy clubs in Boston. Soon, I was driving to New York City and performing in clubs there.

Student 2: Was the money good?

Jay Leno: The money was *horrible*. I used to sleep in alleys behind the clubs. Sometimes I'd sleep in the backseat of my car. *(joking)* I figured it was good training in case I ever had to hide out from the police someday.

Student 2: Then what happened?

Jay Leno: I worked, and worked, and worked. Finally, I started getting noticed. I made my first appearance on *The Tonight Show* in 1975. Over the years, I kept working. I used to be on the road doing shows 300 nights a year. Eventually, I became a guest host on *The Tonight Show*. And then, when Johnny retired, I got the job. It took a lot of work. But I couldn't be happier with the way things turned out.

Student 2: I see our time is gone. Thanks again for being here, Jay.

Jay Leno: Are you kidding? I got to eat school food again! I wouldn't have missed that for the world!

Scene 3

Teacher: Our next guest is also one of the biggest stars on TV, and yet, you might not recognize her. Here's Nancy Cartwright.

Student 3: Hi, Nancy. Our class might not know who you are. But I bet *everyone* knows your work. Tell us what you do.

Nancy Cartwright: *(smiling)* I'm the voice of Bart Simpson, man!

Student 3: Tell us how you got into the business.

Nancy Cartwright: Well, it may seem strange. I always wanted to do voices in cartoons. I knew it when I was ten years old. And as I grew up, I had no idea how to get that kind of work. But my life changed a lot when I was eighteen.

Student 3: How so?

Nancy Cartwright: First of all, my mom died of cancer. So it was a very tough time. I was in college in Ohio. I was also doing character voices on a local radio station. On a whim, I called Daws Butler in California. He was a legend in the cartoon business. He was the voice of Huckleberry Hound, Yogi Bear, and a lot of other famous characters. I thought he might give me some advice.

Student 3: What did he tell you?

Nancy Cartwright: He was impressed with me. He agreed to teach me how to use my voice and get into the business. So I transferred to college in California just to be near him. I didn't know anyone else out west.

Student 3: Then what happened?

Nancy Cartwright: I started getting some work. I was on *Animaniacs* and *Pound Puppies*. I once did seven ponies on *My Little Pony*. Then my big break came.

Student 3: That was *The Simpsons*?

Nancy Cartwright: Right. At first, I read for Lisa's part. That didn't work out so well. Then I read about Bart. I said, "I want to do him." The minute the producers heard the voice, they said, "That's him! That's Bart!" And there's a very good reason why they would choose a woman instead of a boy to do a boy's voice role.

Student 3: What's that?

Nancy Cartwright: As boys grow up, their voices change. Mine won't. Bart's going to be ten years old forever. And I'll do him as long as he's around. It's a great job!

Student 3: Thanks, Nancy. One more thing: can you do Bart's voice for us now?

Nancy Cartwright: *(as Bart Simpson)* No way, man!

Student 3: Thank you, Nancy!

Scene 4

Teacher: Our last guest has spent his whole life serving his country. Please welcome former Senator Bob Dole.

Student 4: Senator Dole, tell us about your childhood.

Bob Dole: I was born in Russell, Kansas, way back in 1923. My father ran a creamery company. My mother gave sewing lessons. I grew up during the Great Depression. Lots of people had no jobs then. Money was scarce for everyone. In fact, at one point, we moved into our basement and rented out the rest of the house. Times were very hard.

Student 4: You also served in World War II, didn't you?

Bob Dole: Yes. I enlisted in the Army in 1942. I saw a lot of action. I was in Italy near the end of the war. We got into a big battle and I was shot in the upper back and right arm. In fact, my arm was shot up so bad that you couldn't even tell it was an arm anymore.

Student 4: Wow. Then what happened?

Bob Dole: It took three years and nine operations to rebuild my arm and shoulder. Still, they couldn't fix the all the damage that had been done. I had to learn how to do everything left-handed. Like how to write, eat, dress myself.

Student 4: How did that change your life?

Bob Dole: I had always dreamed of becoming a doctor. I knew I wouldn't be able to do that anymore. So instead, I got a law degree. A few years later, I got into politics. I served as a state legislator in Kansas from 1951 to 1953.

Student 4: But you didn't stop there, did you?

Bob Dole: No, I didn't. In 1960, I was elected to the U.S. House of Representatives. I served four terms there, and then ran for Senate in 1968. I was a senator from 1968 to 1996.

Student 4: What did you do then?

Bob Dole: In 1996, I left the Senate to run for president. I didn't win, but I got to travel all over our great country and meet many wonderful people. It was a great experience.

Student 4: One last question. What do you do today?

Bob Dole: I work for several charity groups. I still write opinion pieces for major newspapers. And I still try to make a difference in people's lives.

Student 4: Senator Dole, thank you for coming. And thank you for your many years of service to our country.

Bob Dole: Thank you very much.

Teacher: And thanks to all our guests!

Cross Outs

Special Guests

	A	B	C
1	Boston	Alaska	always
2	Bart	Italy	believe
3	in	Ohio	your
4	New York	dreams	poetry

1. Cross out the cities where Jay Leno performed in college in column A.

2. Cross out the country where Bob Dole was injured in row 2.

3. Cross out the U.S. states in which Nancy Cartwright and Jewel lived in column B.

4. Cross out the kind of book Jewel wrote in column C.

5. Cross out the character Nancy Cartwright plays in row 2.

Write the remaining words in order below.

_____ _____ _____ _____

_____.

They All Beat the Odds

Chris Burke (Actor), Patty Duke (Actress), Michelle Akers (Soccer Player), and Stephen Hawking (Scientist)

Summary

This script is presented as a panel of famous people who have had challenges. Chris Burke, an actor, has Down syndrome. Patty Duke, also an actor, battles bipolar disorder. Michelle Akers's soccer career suffered due to chronic fatigue syndrome. And Stephen Hawking has continued his brilliant research despite having ALS, amyotrophic lateral sclerosis, which is also called Lou Gehrig's disease. This script provides a model that could be for students to develop short scripts about other people who have beaten the odds. (See list of useful Web sites on the next page.)

Presentation Suggestions

The organization is slightly different in this script. Rather than having the narrators alternate their reading, each narrator is paired with one guest, as if in an interview. This model could be used by students to work in pairs and develop similar short script segments. The stage can be set so that each narrator is sitting alongside his guest, in a conversational setting.

Related Books and Media

- Kaminsky, Marty. *Uncommon Champions: Fifteen Athletes Who Battled Back.* Honesdale, PA: Boyds Mill Press, 2000.

- McDaniel, Jo Beth, and Chris Burke. *A Special Kind of Hero: Chris Burke's Own Story.* Iuniverse.com, 2001.

- List of biographies and autobiographies about people who beat the odds: http://sachem. suffolk.lib.ny.us/advisor/Bios/bioadversity.htm

- List of famous people with disabilities: http://www.disabled-world.com

- Stephen Hawking Web site: http://www.hawking.org.uk

Characters

Narrator 1

Chris Burke, *actor*

Narrator 2

Patty Duke, *actor*

Narrator 3

Michelle Akers, *soccer player*

Narrator 4

Stephen Hawking, *physicist*

They All Beat the Odds

Scene 1

Narrator 1: Today we have a great group of guests. Each one is a success. Yet each one has faced problems. Each one has beat the odds and found success. Our first guest is Chris Burke. You have probably seen Chris on *Life Goes On* or *Touched by an Angel*. Mr. Burke, please tell us about the challenges you faced.

Chris Burke: I was born with Down syndrome. People with Down syndrome can have a lot of problems. They may be smaller than most people. Some have a hearing loss. People with Down syndrome may have more eye problems than other people.

Narrator 1: How can a person with Down syndrome stay healthy?

Chris Burke: I go to the doctor often. Anyone should see their doctor when sick. But my parents made sure I got to the right doctors.

Narrator 1: I read that one doctor said your parents should not take you home after you were born.

Chris Burke: That's right. The doctor said they couldn't take care of me. But my parents treated me like the other kids. Sometimes kids with Down syndrome are treated like they are dumb. But many can go to school. Many have jobs.

Narrator 1: What do you like to do best?

Chris Burke: I love acting. I am lucky that I get to do what I love. And I get paid for it!

Narrator 1: You've gotten a lot of awards. There's even a school named for you. Where is it?

Chris Burke: It's in New York City.

Narrator 1: I have one last question, Chris. What do you want to do next?

Chris Burke: I would like to do more TV shows and movies. I want to direct some plays for people with disabilities too. I want all kinds of people to have a chance to act.

Narrator 1: Thank you for talking with us today. We will enjoy seeing you on the small screen and the big screen!

Scene 2

Narrator 2: Our next guest is also a television and movie star. She has a different challenge. Patty Duke has bipolar disorder. This is sometimes known as manic depression. Miss Duke, we are glad you came today. Can you tell us about manic depression?

Patty Duke: People with manic depression can feel great one minute and rotten the next. When feeling manic, the world is great. You're full of energy. You feel like you can't do anything wrong. And then, all of a sudden, you feel depressed. You probably know what it's like to feel a bit depressed. We all have those days when we feel a little "blue." But this depression is deep.

Narrator 2: So you would have high highs and low lows.

Patty Duke: That's right. The hard part is that there is not much in between those two feelings. You'd be high—or you'd be low. I didn't find out what was wrong until I was an adult.

Narrator 2: Did anyone else in your family have problems like this?

Patty Duke: My mother probably had the same thing. My dad was an alcoholic. They fought a lot. It was hard growing up in our house.

Narrator 2: How did you get into acting?

Patty Duke: My older brother was acting. I was only thirteen when I got a role in the stage show of *The Miracle Worker*. I played Helen Keller. In 1962 I acted in the movie version. I won an Oscar for that movie. I was sixteen years old.

Narrator 2: Tell us about your TV show.

Patty Duke: I had my own show called "The Patty Duke Show." I played two parts at once. I was a teen in the United States. I was also a cousin in England. It wasn't a good time for me. I needed to get away from my managers. So I got married at age eighteen. I just wanted to get away.

Narrator 2: What happened after you got married?

Patty Duke: It didn't solve my problems. That's for sure! I tried drugs. I drank too much alcohol. I even tried to kill myself. Finally, I got a divorce.

Narrator 2: You married again, didn't you?

Patty Duke: I married two more times before marrying John Astin. We had two sons.

Narrator 2: When did you find out what was wrong with you?

Patty Duke: I found out in 1982. It was such a relief! Lithium is a drug that works for a lot of people with bipolar disorder. I am lucky. It is perfect for me.

Narrator 2: Do you have any final thoughts or advice for us?

Patty Duke: If you think you have problems with depression, get help! Don't wait. Help is out there for you.

Narrator 2: Thanks for being so open with us today, Miss Duke. I know we've learned a lot.

Scene 3

Narrator 3: Now we turn to the world of sports for our next guest. Michelle Akers is one of the best soccer players ever. She played against lots of players on the soccer field. But she also had to battle back from illness. Welcome, Ms. Akers. Can you tell us what you were like as a kid?

Michelle Akers: Thank you for having me here. Well, as a kid, let's just say I had a lot of energy! I loved playing any sport that had a ball. No dolls for me.

Narrator 3: How did you start playing soccer?

Michelle Akers: We moved to Seattle. I joined a league there. I was good so they made me goalie. Then they realized I could score goals. So that ended my being a goalie. I was tall in high school. That helped a lot. I could use my head to get balls into the net.

Narrator 3: When did you start playing for the U.S. team?

Michelle Akers: The first women's national team was started in 1985. I was invited to try out. And I made the team.

Narrator 3: When did things start to go wrong?

Michelle Akers: We had won our first World Cup in 1991. I was exhausted. I started getting migraine headaches. I'd have to go to bed a lot. I was dizzy. I couldn't eat much. I was so sick that I wanted to die.

Narrator 3: What was the problem?

Michelle Akers: They weren't sure at first. Finally they figured out I had CFS or chronic fatigue syndrome. It means you're always tired—very tired. And going to bed to get some rest doesn't fix it.

Narrator 3: But you kept playing for a long time.

Michelle Akers: I didn't want to give in. Or give up. So I'd rest and play as much as I could. We changed my position so I didn't have to run as hard.

Narrator 3: What about when you were off the field? What was life like?

Michelle Akers: I changed my diet. I ended a marriage that was making me unhappy. And I found that my faith helped a lot.

Narrator 3: Thank you, Michelle. I know you'll keep playing a great game no matter what you do.

Scene 4

Narrator 4: Our last guest is Dr. Stephen William Hawking. He isn't someone you'd see in the movies or on the soccer field. He is in a wheelchair and he needs help speaking to us. But he is very famous. He studied physics. He works on the laws of science. For example, he studies space, time, and black holes. He is a gifted writer. He has received many honors for his research. Dr. Hawking also speaks to people a lot. Welcome, Dr. Hawking.

Stephen Hawking: It's good to be here. I've always wanted to rub elbows with movie and sports stars!

Narrator 4: We know that you got a disease with a very long name. It's called amyotrophic lateral sclerosis.

Stephen Hawking: Let's make things easy. We'll call this ALS.

Narrator 4: I've read that you were a clumsy kid. You were in college when you got worse. Can you tell us how you found out you had it?

Stephen Hawking: I'd just fall over. I got lots of tests. Then I found out that I had ALS.

Narrator 4: You found out that ALS couldn't be cured. Your muscles were going to stop functioning. And that it would probably kill you in a few years. How did you handle that?

Stephen Hawking: I had a lot of dreams. One dream seemed to tell me I could help others. I decided I had to try to keep going.

Narrator 4: But you didn't die like they thought you would.

Stephen Hawking: I'll tell you what helped. I met Jane Wilde. We got married. So I had to earn a living!

Narrator 4: You have done some important research. You have written many papers and books.

Stephen Hawking: I get lots of help with my work.

Narrator 4: You speak with the help of a computer program and a synthesizer. Has that been important?

Stephen Hawking: ALS gives me slurred speech. With this help, I can sound normal.

Narrator 4: For my last question, could you share what you are most thankful for?

Stephen Hawking: I have a great wife and three great kids. I've been lucky. The ALS has gotten worse very slowly. Just like in my dream, I needed to help others. My research has done that. I hope to be around to help a lot more.

Narrator 4: We hope all of you will be here for many years. We thank all our guests for coming today. You have all beaten the odds!

Cross Outs

They All Beat the Odds

	A	B	C
1	space	you	time
2	depression	can	Down Syndrome
3	beat	CFS	the
4	odds	ALS	too

1. Cross out the name of Chris Burke's challenge in column C.

2. Cross out the name of Patty Duke's challenge in row 2.

3. Cross out the initials for Stephen Hawking's challenge in column B.

4. Cross out the initials for Michelle Akers's challenge in row 3.

5. Cross out the two things that Stephen Hawking studies in row 1.

Write the remaining words in order below.

_____ _____ _____ _____

_____ _____.

Answers to Cross Out Puzzles

Angle: Wrestlers pin hopes on winning.

Armstrong: Beating cancer takes hard work.

Baiul: Some skaters live on edge.

Berry: Halle opens doors for women of color.

Bocelli: Singing is Andrea's biggest dream.

Brosnihan: Say yes I can to life.

Bruschi: Champions never give up.

Cruise: Tom cruises to acting success.

Diesel: Be determined, persistent, and confident.

Driscoll: Jean runs on wheels to win.

Eckstein: Short Angel beats Giants.

Fox: Fox acts up and speaks out.

Garrison: Win the game with good health.

Gold: Good health is a treasure.

Hamilton: Have faith in your abilities.

McCarthy: Overcome tragedy and find success.

McGraw: The McGraws score big hits.

O'Ree: Hockey players reach their goals.

Prinze Jr.: Freddie Prinze Jr. finds super strength.

Reeve: Determination is a super power.

Roosevelt: Great strength comes from within.

Weihenmayer: Reach the heights of success.

Woodruff: Bob doesn't let a blast stop him.

Special Guests: Always believe in your dreams.

They All Beat the Odds: You can beat the odds too.

Index

About the Authors

SUZANNE I. BARCHERS, Ed.D., has written more than fifty books, ranging from college textbooks to children's books. She has served as a public school teacher, an affiliate faculty for the University of Colorado—Denver, acquisitions editor for Teacher Ideas Press, Managing Editor at *Weekly Reader,* and Editor in Chief and Vice President of LeapFrog. She also serves on the PBS Kids Media Advisory Board and the board of directors for the Association of Educational Publishers (EdPress). Recent titles from the Suzanne include: *Classic Readers Theatre for Young Adults* (2002), *Judge for Yourself: Famous American Trials for Readers Theatre* (2004), *More Readers Theatre for Beginning Readers* (2006), and *Getting Ready to Read with Readers Theatre* (2007).

MICHAEL RUSCOE is a writer, journalist, teacher, and the author of several books, including *Baseball: A Treasury of Art and Literature*. He lives in Connecticut with his wife, his son Benjamin, and his daughter Abigail.